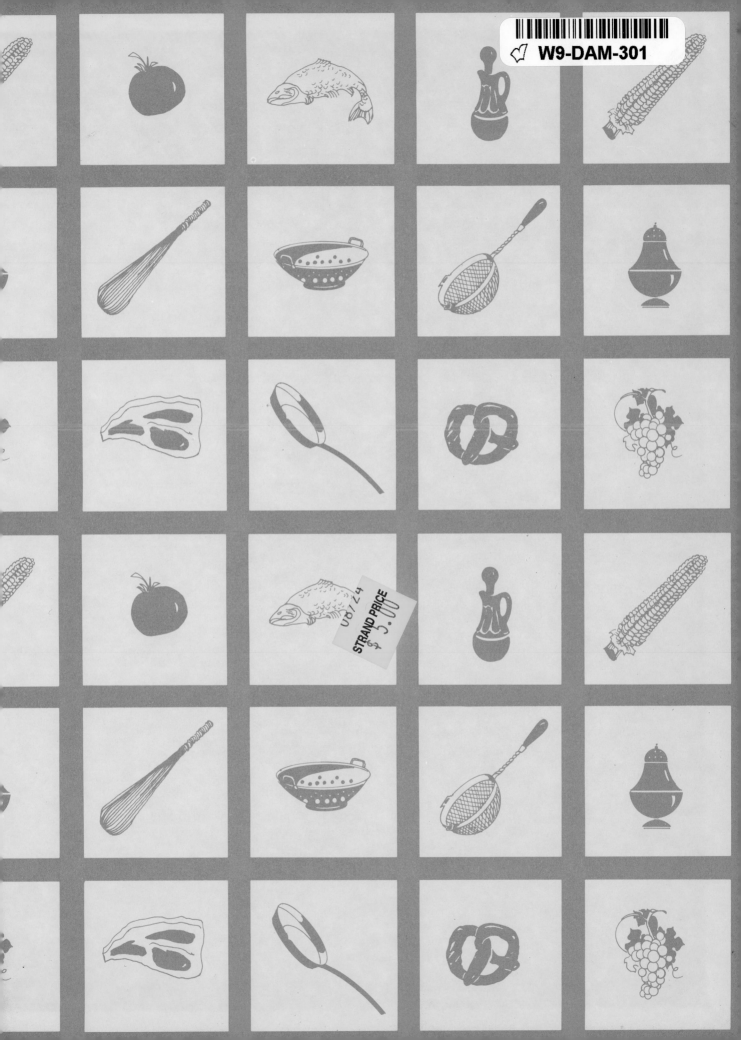

ILLUSTRATED LIBRARY OF COOKING

TIME LIFE BOOKS

ILLUSTRATED LIBRARY OF COOKING

Vegetables

Culinary Arts Institute®
A DIVISION OF DELAIR PUBLISHING COMPANY

Published, under agreement with Time-Life Books, by
Culinary Arts Institute
a division of
Delair Publishing Company, Inc.
420 Lexington Avenue
New York, New York 10170

These recipes were previously published in a
different format by Time-Life Books.

The Time-Life Illustrated Library of Cooking
is a collection of tested recipes
by leading authorities in the world of cooking.
This volume contains recipes
by the experts listed below:

Michael Field, the consulting editor
for the Foods of the World series,
was one of America's top-ranking cooking experts
and a contributor to leading magazines.

James A. Beard, a renowned authority
on American cuisine, is also
an accomplished teacher and writer
of the culinary arts.

Allison Williams is the author
of *The Embassy Cookbook*,
her collection of authentic recipes
from various embassies in Washington.

ISBN: 0-8326-0804-1

Stuffed Artichoke Hearts

Fonds d' Artichauts Farcis   *To serve 8*

8 cooked or canned artichoke hearts
1½ teaspoons salt
½ teaspoon pepper
6 tablespoons butter
¼ cup minced onions
¼ cup minced celery
¼ cup minced carrots
1 cup chopped mushrooms

1. Scoop out the choke, or prickly center, of the artichoke hearts, then sprinkle the hearts with half the salt and pepper.
2. Melt half the butter in a casserole. Add the artichokes and simmer them for 5 minutes, basting frequently.
3. Preheat the oven to 325°.
4. Melt the remaining butter in a skillet and sauté the onions, celery, carrots and mushrooms for 8 minutes.
5. Mix well, and season them with the remaining salt and pepper.
6. Stuff the artichoke hearts with the sautéed vegetables.
7. Return them to the casserole, cover with a piece of buttered wax paper, and bake for 20 minutes.

Artichokes in Dill Sauce

Anginares a la Polita   *To serve 6*

½ cup fresh lemon juice
¼ cup flour
1 cup flour
1 cup water
6 medium-sized artichokes
1 cup olive oil
½ cup finely chopped onions
¼ cup finely cut fresh dill, or substitute 1
  tablespoon dried dill weed
2 teaspoons salt

1. In a large, deep bowl, beat the lemon juice and flour together with a whisk or spoon, add the water and beat to a smooth thin paste. Set aside.
2. With a small, sharp knife, trim ⅛ inch off the stem end of each artichoke and peel the tough outer skin from the remaining stem. Snap off the small bottom leaves and any bruised or discolored outer leaves.
3. Lay each artichoke on its side, grip it firmly, and with a large knife slice about 1 inch off the top. Spread the top leaves apart gently and pull out the inner core of thistlelike yellow leaves.
4. With a long-handled spoon, scrape out the hairy choke inside.
5. Drop the artichokes into the lemon-juice mixture, turning them about to coat them evenly and let them soak while you make the sauce.
6. Heat the olive oil over moderate heat in a shallow enameled or stainless-steel casserole large enough to hold the artichokes comfortably.
7. Add the onions and cook for 5 minutes, or until they are soft and transparent but not brown.
8. Drain the artichoke-soaking liquid into the casserole, add the dill and salt and, stirring constantly, bring to a boil over high heat.
9. Lay the artichokes side by side in the sauce and baste them thoroughly.
10. Reduce the heat to low, cover tightly, and simmer for 20 minutes.
11. Then turn the artichokes over and, basting occasionally, simmer 25 minutes longer, or until their bases show no resistance when pierced with the point of a small knife.
12. Remove from the heat and let the artichokes cool to room temperature.
13. To serve, arrange on a platter and spoon the sauce over them.

Baked Stuffed Artichokes

Carciofi al Tegame alla Romana   *To serve 4*

**4 small artichokes, about 6 to 8 ounces
    each**
Lemon juice
6 quarts water
6 tablespoons olive oil
**1½ cups fresh white bread crumbs (made
    from French or Italian bread)**
1½ teaspoons finely chopped garlic
4 teaspoons wine vinegar
**1½ teaspoons crumbled dried mint leaves,
    without the stems or 1 tablespoon finely
    chopped fresh mint**
1 teaspoon salt
Freshly ground black pepper

1. Trim the bases of the artichokes flush and flat so they can stand upright. (As you cut them, rub these and all the rest of the cut edges with lemon juice to prevent discoloring.)
2. Bend and snap off the small bottom leaves and any outer leaves that are bruised or loose.
3. Lay each artichoke on its side, grip it firmly, and slice about 1 inch off the top.
4. With scissors, trim ¼ inch off the points of the leaves.
5. In a large enameled kettle or soup pot, bring 6 quarts of water to a bubbling boil over high heat.
6. Drop in the artichokes and cook them for 10 minutes, then drain and cool them upside down in a colander or large sieve.
7. Now gently spread the top leaves of each one apart and pull out the tender inner core of thistlelike yellow leaves.
8. With a long-handled spoon (iced-tea spoon size is ideal) carefully and thoroughly scrape out the hairy choke inside to leave the heart clean.
9. Brush a few drops of lemon juice inside each artichoke.
10. Preheat the oven to 350°.
11. Heat the oil in a heavy 8- to 10-inch skillet. Add the bread crumbs and cook them over moderate heat, stirring constantly, for 1 or 2 minutes, or until they are crisp and barely colored.
12. Remove the pan from the heat and stir in the garlic. Then mix in the vinegar, mint, salt and a few grindings of pepper.
13. Spoon about 2 tablespoons of stuffing into the center of each artichoke.
14. With your fingers, press the rest of the stuffing between the larger outer leaves of the artichokes.
15. Arrange the artichokes snugly in a deep 8- or 9-inch baking dish and pour in boiling water to a depth of 1 inch.
16. Cover the dish tightly, with foil if necessary, and bake on the middle shelf of the oven for 1 hour, or until the bases of the artichokes are tender when pierced with the tip of a sharp knife.
17. Serve them or brush them with olive oil and serve cold with quartered lemons.

To trim an artichoke before cooking, use a sharp knife to cut an inch or so off the top cone of leaves.

Then, using kitchen scissors, clip the sharp point off each of the artichoke's large outer leaves.

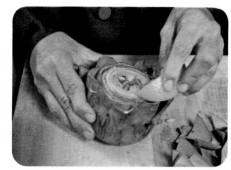

As you trim, rub all the cut edges of the leaves with lemon juice to prevent them from discoloring.

Asparagus Marinated in Soybean Paste

Karashi Zuke   *To serve 2 to 4*

6 slender young asparagus stalks, peeled
½ cup *shiro miso* (white soybean paste)
1 tablespoon powdered mustard

TO COOK AND ASSEMBLE: 1. Snap the tips from the asparagus and save for future use. Slice the stalks lengthwise into strips ½ inch wide, then cut these into 1½-inch lengths.
2. Over high heat, bring 2 cups of water to a boil. Add the asparagus, return to the boil, and drain immediately in a sieve. Run cold water over them to cool them quickly, and pat dry with paper towels.
3. In a small mixing bowl, combine the *miso* with the dry mustard and mix until smooth.
4. Spread half the mixture in a shallow baking dish or casserole and cover with a double thickness of cheesecloth the size of the dish.
5. Place the asparagus in one layer on the cheesecloth and cover with another double thickness of cheesecloth.
6. Top with the remaining *miso* and mustard mixture.
7. Marinate for about 3 hours at room temperature, or refrigerate overnight.
8. Discard the dressing before serving the asparagus.

Green Beans in Tomato Sauce

Judías Verdes con Salsa de Tomate   *To serve 4*

1 teaspoon salt
1 pound fresh green string beans, trimmed
and cut into 2-inch lengths
2 tablespoons olive oil
¼ cup finely chopped onions
1 teaspoon finely chopped garlic
4 medium-sized tomatoes, peeled, seeded
and finely chopped, or substitute 1½
cups chopped, drained, canned tomatoes
1 tablespoon finely chopped parsley
2 teaspoons sugar
Freshly ground black pepper

1. In a heavy 3- to 4-quart saucepan, bring the salt and 2 quarts of water to a boil over high heat.
2. Drop in the beans, a handful at a time. Bring to a boil again, reduce the heat to moderate and boil uncovered for 10 to 15 minutes until the beans are barely tender.
3. Drain a colander and set the beans aside.
4. Heat the olive oil in a heavy 10- to 12-inch skillet until a light haze forms above it.
5. Add the onions and garlic and, stirring frequently, cook over moderate heat for 5 minutes, or until the onions are soft and transparent but not brown.
6. Stir in the tomatoes, parsley, sugar and a few grindings of pepper, bring to a boil, and cook, uncovered, until most of the liquid evaporates and the mixture is thick enough to hold its shape lightly in a spoon.
7. Stir in the beans and simmer for a minute or two until they are heated through.
8. Taste for seasoning and serve at once from a heated bowl.

Green Beans Paprika

To serve 4

2 quarts water
1 teaspoon salt
1 pound green beans, cut into 1-inch
 pieces (about 3 cups)
4 tablespoons butter
¾ cup finely chopped onions
1 tablespoon sweet Hungarian paprika
2 tablespoons flour
1 cup sour cream
½ teaspoon salt

1. In a 3-quart saucepan or soup kettle, bring 2 quarts of water and a teaspoon of salt to a bubbling boil over high heat.
2. Drop the beans in by the handful.
3. Bring the water to a boil again, reduce the heat to medium and cook the beans, uncovered, for 10 to 15 minutes, or until they are just tender. Drain them immediately in a sieve or colander.
4. Melt the butter in a heavy 10-inch skillet, and when the foam subsides, add the onions. Cook for 4 or 5 minutes, or until they are translucent.
5. Off the heat, stir in the paprika, continuing to stir until the onions are well coated.
6. With a wire whisk, beat the flour into the sour cream, then stir the mixture into the skillet with the onions and add the salt.
7. Simmer on low heat for 4 or 5 minutes, or until the sauce is smooth and creamy.
8. Gently stir in the beans; simmer about 5 minutes longer, or until heated through.

Buttered Green Beans

Haricots Verts au Naturel *To serve 6 to 8*

6 quarts water
3 tablespoons salt
3 pounds green string beans, trimmed
2 tablespoons butter
Salt
Freshly ground black pepper

1. In a large kettle or soup pot, bring the water and 3 tablespoons of salt to a bubbling boil over high heat.
2. Drop the beans in by the handful.
3. Return the water to a boil, reduce the heat to moderate and boil the beans uncovered for 10 to 15 minutes, or until they are just tender. Do not overcook them.
4. Immediately drain them in a large sieve or colander.
5. If the beans are to be served at once, melt 2 tablespoons of butter in a 2- to 3-quart saucepan and toss the beans with the butter for a minute or two, season them with salt and pepper, then transfer them to a serving dish.
6. If the beans are to be served later, refresh them after they have been drained by quickly plunging the sieve or colander into a large pot of cold water and letting it remain there for 2 or 3 minutes.
7. Drain the beans thoroughly, place them in a bowl, cover and set aside – in the refrigerator if they are to wait for long.
8. If you plan to serve them hot, reheat them in 2 tablespoons of hot butter, season them and let them warm through over moderate heat.

Swedish Brown Beans

Bruna Bönor *To serve 4*

1¾ cups imported Swedish dried brown
 beans
5 cups water
1½ teaspoons salt
½ cup white vinegar
½ cup dark corn syrup
1 tablespoon dark brown sugar

1. Wash the beans thoroughly in cold running water. Since the beans will expand considerably as they soak, put them in a large pot with 5 cups of cold water.

2. Bring to a boil, turn off the heat and let the beans soak, uncovered, for at least 1 hour (or you may soak them overnight in cold water and omit the boiling process).

3. Whichever method you choose to cook the beans, bring the soaked beans to a boil in their soaking water, then half cover the pot and simmer over very low heat for 1 hour.

4. Stir in the salt, vinegar, corn syrup and brown sugar, and continue cooking slowly. The beans should be tender in another hour, and the sauce should be brown and thick. However, dried beans vary enormously in their moisture content, and the cooking time may be longer or shorter by as much as half an hour. To make certain that the beans do not overcook, test by eating one occasionally.

5. If the cooking liquid evaporates too much before the beans are done, add a little water. If, on the other hand, the sauce has not thickened sufficiently by the time the beans are almost done, boil them rapidly, uncovered, over high heat to reduce the liquid.

Cranberry Beans with Squash and Corn

Porotos Granados   *To serve 6*

3 cups shelled fresh cranberry beans
5 cups cold water
¼ cup olive oil
1½ cups coarsely chopped onions
½ teaspoon finely chopped garlic
6 medium tomatoes, peeled, seeded, chopped
1½ teaspoons dried basil
1 teaspoon dried oregano
Freshly ground black pepper
1 pound winter squash, peeled, seeded and cut into 1-inch cubes (about 2 cups)
½ cup fresh corn kernels, cut from 1 large ear or corn, or substitute ½ cup thoroughly defrosted frozen corn kernels
1 teaspoon salt

1. Rinse the beans under cold running water and combine them with 5 cups of water in a heavy 5-quart casserole.

2. Bring to a boil, reduce the heat to low and let the beans simmer, half-covered.

3. In a heavy 8- to 10-inch skillet heat the oil over moderate heat.

4. Add the onions and garlic, and cook, stirring occasionally, for 5 minutes, or until the onions are soft and transparent but not brown.

5. Stir in the tomatoes, basil, oregano and a few grindings of pepper, raise the heat and boil briskly, stirring, until the mixture becomes a thick purée.

6. Add the purée and the squash to the simmering beans.

7. Cover and cook over low heat for 1½ to 2 hours.

8. When the beans are tender, stir in the corn, and simmer 5 minutes.

9. Season with salt, and transfer the beans to a serving bowl.

10. Serve hot in soup plates.

NOTE: If fresh cranberry beans are unavailable, substitute 1½ cups of dried cranberry or navy beans. Rinse them, bring to a boil in 6 cups of water, and boil for 2 minutes. Turn off the heat and let the beans soak for an hour. Add the purée and squash and proceed with the recipe.

Refried Beans

Frijoles Refritos   *To serve 4 to 6*

2 cups dried pink beans or dried red kidney beans
6 cups cold water
1 cup coarsely chopped onions
2 medium tomatoes, peeled, seeded and coarsely chopped, or substitute ⅔ cup chopped, drained, canned Italian plum tomatoes
½ teaspoon finely chopped garlic
1 teaspoon crumbled and seeded dried *pequín* chili
¼ teaspoon crumbled *epazote*, if available
¼ teaspoon freshly ground black pepper
½ cup lard
1 teaspoon salt

NOTE: Wear rubber gloves when handling the hot chilies.

1. Place the beans in a colander or sieve and run cold water over them until the draining water runs clear. Pick out and discard any black or shriveled beans.

2. In a 3-quart heavy pot, combine the water, ½ cup of the onions, ¼ cup of the tomatoes, ¼ teaspoon of the garlic, the chili, *epazote* (if used) and pepper, and drop in the beans.

3. Bring the water to a boil over high heat, then half-cover the pan and reduce the heat to low.

4. Simmer the beans for about 15 minutes and stir in 1 tablespoon of the lard.

5. Simmer, half covered, for 1½ hours, add the teaspoon of salt, and over the lowest possible heat, simmer for another 30 minutes, or until the beans are very tender and have absorbed all their cooking liquid.

6. During the last half hour of cooking, stir the beans gently now and then to prevent their sticking to the bottom of the pan.

7. Remove the pan from the heat, and cover it to keep the beans warm.

8. In a heavy 12-inch skillet, melt 2 more tablespoons of the lard over high heat until a light haze forms above it.

9. Add the remaining chopped onions and garlic, and turn the heat down to moderate, then fry for about 5 minutes, or until the onions are transparent but not brown.

10. Stir in the remaining tomatoes and simmer for 2 or 3 minutes.

11. Fry the cooked beans in the following fashion: Add 3 tablespoons of the beans to the pan of simmering sauce, mash them with a fork, then stir in 1 tablespoon of the remaining lard. Continue adding and mashing the beans in similar amounts, following each addition with another tablespoon of lard until all the beans and lard have been used.

12. Cook over low heat for 10 minutes, stirring frequently, until the beans are fairly dry.

13. To serve, transfer the beans to a serving bowl or individual dishes. *Frijoles refritos* are a traditional accompaniment to tortilla dishes.

Beans with Fruit and Vegetables

Westfälisches Blindhuhn   *To serve 4 to 6*

1 quart cold water
1 cup dried white beans, preferably Great
   Northern or navy beans
½ pound slab of lean bacon cut lengthwise
   into 3 strips and crosswise into halves
1½ pounds cooking apples and 1½ pounds
   firm ripe pears, peeled, cored and cut into ¼-inch wedges, or use 3 pounds of
   cooking apples, peeled, cored and cut into ¼-inch wedges
1 pound fresh green string beans, trimmed
   and cut into 2-inch lengths
1 cup coarsely diced scraped carrots
3 medium-sized boiling potatoes (about 1
   pound), peeled and cut ½-inch dice
Salt
Freshly ground black pepper

1. In a heavy 4- to 6-quart saucepan or soup pot, bring 1 quart of water to a bubbling boil over high heat.

2. Drop in the dried beans and boil uncovered for 2 minutes. Turn off the heat and let the beans soak for 1 hour.

3. Then add the bacon, return the beans to a boil, and reduce the heat to low.

4. Partially cover the pan and simmer as slowly as possible for about 1 hour, or until the beans are barely tender.

5. Add the apples, pears, green beans, carrots, potatoes, salt to taste and a few grindings of pepper to the beans.

6. Partially cover the pan and simmer, stirring occasionally, for 30 minutes longer, or until the vegetables and fruit are tender and the beans fully cooked.

7. Taste for seasoning and serve hot from a deep heated bowl.

White beans and lean bacon are combined with string beans, carrots, potatoes, apples and pears in this colorful German vegetable dish called "blind hen."

White Beans with Tomatoes and Garlic

Fagioli all' Uccelletto   *To serve 4 to 6*

3 cups canned *cannellini* or other white
  beans (1½ one-pound cans); or 1½ cups
  dry white kidney, marrow, Great Northern
  or navy beans and 1½ quarts water
¼ cup olive oil
1 teaspoon finely chopped garlic
¼ teaspoon sage leaves, crumbled
2 large ripe tomatoes, peeled, seeded,
  gently squeezed of excess juice, and
  coarsely chopped
½ teaspoon salt
Freshly ground black pepper
1 tablespoon wine vinegar

1. If you are using dry beans, combine them with the water in a 3- to 4-quart saucepan and bring them to a boil over high heat.
2. Boil briskly for 2 minutes, remove the pan from the heat and let the beans soak for 1 hour.
3. Now bring the water to a boil again, turn the heat down to low, and simmer the beans for 1 to 1½ hours, or until they are tender; drain and set aside.
4. If you are using canned beans, drain them in a large sieve or colander, or wash them under cold running water, then set them aside in the sieve or colander.
5. In a heavy 8- to 10-inch skillet, heat the oil until a light haze forms over it.
6. Add the garlic and sage and cook, stirring, for 30 seconds.
7. Stir in the drained beans, tomatoes, salt and a few grindings of pepper.
8. Cover and simmer over low heat for 10 minutes.
9. Taste for seasoning, then stir in the vinegar.
10. Serve in a heated bowl or on a deep platter.

Boston Baked Beans

To Serve 6 to 8

4 cups dried pea or Great Northern beans
2 teaspoons salt
2 medium-sized whole onions, peeled
4 cloves
½ cup molasses
1 cup brown sugar
2 teaspoons dry mustard
1 teaspoon black pepper
2 cups water
½ pound salt pork, scored

1. Put the beans in a large saucepan and pour in enough cold water to cover them by at least 2 inches.
2. Bring to a boil, let boil for 2 minutes, then let the beans soak in the water off the heat for about 1 hour.
3. Bring them to a boil again, add 1 teaspoon of the salt, half cover the pan and simmer the beans as slowly as possible for about 30 minutes, or until they are partially done.
4. Drain the beans and discard the bean water.
5. Preheat the oven to 250°.
6. To bake the beans, choose a traditional 4-quart bean pot or a heavy casserole with a tight-fitting cover.
7. Place 2 onions, each stuck with 2 cloves, in the bottom of the bean pot or casserole and cover with the beans.
8. In a small mixing bowl, combine the molasses, ¾ cup of the brown sugar, mustard, and 1 teaspoon each of salt and black pepper.
9. Slowly stirring with a large spoon, pour in the 2 cups of water.
10. Pour this mixture over the beans and push the salt pork slightly beneath the surface.
11. Cover tightly and bake in the center of the oven for 4½ to 5 hours.
12. Then remove the cover and sprinkle with the remaining ¼ cup of brown sugar.
13. Bake the beans uncovered for another ½ hour and serve.

Fava Beans with Sausage and Mint

Habas a la Catalana   *To serve 4 to 6*

**1 pound *chorizos*, or other garlic-seasoned
  smoked pork sausage
1 tablespoon lard
¼ pound salt pork finely diced
½ cup finely chopped scallions
1 teaspoon finely chopped garlic
½ cup dry white wine
½ cup water
1 tablespoon finely cut fresh mint
1 small bay leaf, crumbled
½ teaspoon salt
Freshly ground black pepper
4 cups cooked, fresh fava beans or
  substitute drained, canned favas or frozen
  baby lima beans
2 tablespoons finely chopped parsley**

1. Place the sausages in a 8- to 10-inch skillet and prick them in two or three places with the point of a small, sharp knife.
2. Add enough cold water to cover them completely and bring to a boil over high heat.
3. Reduce the heat to low and simmer uncovered for 5 minutes. Drain on paper towels, then slice the sausages into ¼-inch-thick rounds.
4. In a heavy 3- to 4-quart casserole, melt the lard over moderate heat.
5. Add the salt pork and, stirring frequently, cook until the pieces have rendered all their fat and become crisp and golden brown.
6. With a slotted spoon, transfer them to paper towels to drain.
7. Add the scallions and garlic to the fat in the pan and cook for about 5 minutes, or until the scallions are soft but not brown.
8. Pour in the wine and water and add the sliced sausages, pork dice, mint, bay leaf, salt and a few grindings of pepper.
9. Bring to a boil over high heat, reduce the heat to low and simmer partially covered for 20 minutes.

10. Add the beans and parsley and simmer uncovered, stirring frequently, for about 10 minutes longer, or until the beans are heated through.
11. Taste the *habas a la Catalana* for seasoning and serve at once from a heated bowl or a deep heated platter.

Broccoli Braised in White Wine

Broccoli alla Romana   *To serve 4 to 6*

**¼ cup olive oil
1 teaspoon finely chopped garlic
5 to 6 cups fresh broccoli flowerets
  (about 2 pounds fresh broccoli with
  stems)
1½ cups dry white wine
½ teaspoon salt
Freshly ground black pepper**

1. In a heavy 10- to 12-inch skillet, heat the olive oil until a light haze forms over it.
2. Remove the pan from the heat and stir the garlic in the hot oil for 30 seconds.
3. Return to moderate heat and toss the broccoli flowerets in the oil until they glisten.
4. Add the wine, salt and a few grindings of pepper and simmer uncovered, stirring occasionally, for 5 minutes.
5. Then cover the skillet and simmer for another 15 minutes, or until the broccoli is tender.
6. To serve, quickly, transfer the flowerets with a slotted spoon to a heated bowl or deep platter.
7. Briskly boil the liquid left in the skillet over high heat until it has reduced to about ½ cup and pour it over the broccoli.

Brussels Sprouts with Chestnuts

To serve 4

1 pound chestnuts
2 tablespoons butter
2 tablespoons sherry
1 teaspoon meat extract
1 teaspoon tomato paste
2 teaspoons corn starch
1 cup light stock
1 bay leaf
1 pound Brussels sprouts
Lemon juice

1. Cover the chestnuts with cold water, bring to a boil, and boil them for 2 to 3 minutes. Drain, shell and skin them.
2. Heat the butter in a skillet and brown the chestnuts quickly.
3. Pour the sherry over the nuts, then remove them from the pan.
4. Add to the pan juices the meat extract, the tomato paste and the potato flour, then pour in the light stock.
5. Stir over the heat until it is boiling, then return the nuts to the pan and add the bay leaf. Simmer gently until the chestnuts are just soft.
6. In the meantime, boil the Brussels sprouts in salted water with lemon juice added.
7. Drain the sprouts when they are just tender, mix them with the chestnuts, and serve immediately in a heated casserole.

Cabbage in Sweet-and-Sour Sauce

Cavoli in Agrodolce   *To serve 4 to 6*

3 tablespoons olive oil
1/2 cup thinly sliced onions
1 1/2 pounds cabbage, cut into 1/4-inch strips
   (about 8 cups)

3 large tomatoes, peeled, seeded and coarsely chopped
2 tablespoons wine vinegar
2 teaspoons salt
Freshly ground black pepper
1 tablespoon sugar

1. Heat the olive oil in a heavy 10- to 12-inch skillet, add the onions and cook them over moderate heat, stirring constantly, for 2- or 3 minutes. When they are transparent but not brown, stir in the cabbage, tomatoes, vinegar, salt and a few grindings of pepper.
2. Simmer uncovered, stirring frequently, for 20 minutes, or until the cabbage is tender.
3. Then stir the sugar into the cabbage and cook a minute or 2 longer.

Red Cabbage

Rødkaal   *To serve 6 to 8*

4 pounds red cabbage
1/4 pound butter
1 apple, peeled and sliced
1/3 cup vinegar
1 cup red currant juice or 1/2 cup currant
   jelly mixed with 1/2 cup water
1 1/2 teaspoons salt
1/4 cup sugar

1. Wash the cabbage, discarding any tough outer leaves, and shred it fine.
2. Melt the butter in a large, heavy saucepan.
3. Add the cabbage and the sliced apple.
4. Cover and cook for 5 minutes, shaking the pan frequently.
5. Add the vinegar, currant juice, salt and sugar.
6. Cover the pan again and cook over low heat for 2 hours, stirring frequently and adding a little water if necessary.
7. Taste for seasoning – the cabbage should be sweet and sour.

Fresh green cabbage is a versatile vegetable, whether cooked simply in white wine as described below, or made into sauerkraut *(recipes, pages 53-54)*.

Cabbage in White Wine

To serve 6 to 8

8 tablespoons (1 quarter-pound stick)
   butter
3 pounds green cabbage, cored and coarsely chopped
1 cup white wine, such as a California
   Chablis
1 teaspoon fresh tarragon or ½ teaspoon
   dried
1 teaspoon salt
Freshly ground black pepper

1. In a heavy 10- or 12-inch skillet, melt the butter over moderate heat.

2. When the foam subsides, add the cabbage and, with a fork, toss it in the melted butter until it is well coated.

3. Cook uncovered, stirring occasionally, for 10 minutes, then add the wine, tarragon, salt and a few grindings of pepper.

4. Bring to a boil, cover tightly and reduce the heat to low. Simmer for 5 to 10 minutes, or until the cabbage is tender.

5. With a slotted spoon, remove the cabbage from the pan to a heated vegetable dish or platter.

6. Boil the liquid in the pan rapidly, un-covered, for a few minutes to concentrate its flavor before pouring it over the cabbage.

Braised Red Cabbage

Rødkaal   *To serve 6*

1 medium head red cabbage, 2 to 2½
pounds
4 tablespoons butter
1 tablespoon sugar
1 teaspoon salt
⅓ cup water
⅓ cup white vinegar
¼ cup red currant jelly
2 tablespoons grated apple

1. Wash the head of cabbage under cold running water, remove the tough outer leaves, and cut the cabbage in half from top to bottom.
2. Lay the flat sides down on the chopping board, cut away the core and slice the cabbage very finely. There should be approximately 9 cups of shredded cabbage when you finish.
3. Preheat the oven to 325°.
4. Combine the butter, sugar, salt, water and vinegar in a heavy stainless-steel or enameled 4- to 5-quart casserole.
5. When it comes to a boil and the butter has melted, add the shredded cabbage and toss thoroughly with two wooden spoons or forks.
6. Bring to a boil again, cover tightly and place in the center of the oven to braise for 2 hours. There is little danger that the cabbage will dry out during the cooking, but it is a good idea to check the liquid level occasionally. Add a little water if it seems necessary.
7. About 10 minutes before the cabbage is finished, stir in the jelly and grated apple, replace the cover and complete the cooking.
8. The piquant taste of red cabbage will improve if, after it has cooked, it is allowed to rest for a day in the refrigerator and then reheated either on top of the stove or in a 325° oven.

Glazed Carrots

Carrottes Glacés   *To serve 4 to 6*

10 to 12 medium carrots, peeled and cut
in 2-inch cylinders or olive shapes
1½ cups beef or chicken stock, fresh or
canned
4 tablespoons butter
2 tablespoons sugar
½ teaspoon salt
Freshly ground black pepper
2 tablespoons finely chopped, fresh parsley

1. In a heavy 8- to 10-inch skillet, bring the carrots, stock, butter, sugar, salt and a few grindings of pepper to a boil over moderate heat.
2. Then cover and simmer over low heat, shaking the skillet occasionally to roll the carrots about in the liquid. Check to see that the liquid is not cooking away too fast; if it is, add more stock.
3. In 20 to 30 minutes the carrots should be tender when pierced with the tip of a sharp knife, and the braising liquid should be a brown, syrupy glaze.
4. If the stock has not reduced enough, remove the carrots to a plate and boil the liquid down over high heat.
5. Before serving, roll the carrots around in the pan to coat them with the glaze.
6. Transfer the carrots to a heated vegetable dish, and sprinkle them with fresh parsley.

NOTE: This technique may also be used for parsnips and for white and yellow turnips.

Cauliflower with Sesame Sauce

Karnabeet Makly   *To serve 4 to 6*

1 large cauliflower (about 2 to 2½ pounds)
1 teaspoon salt
Vegetable oil or shortening for deep frying
Sesame sauce (below)

1. Cut away the thick stem at the base of the cauliflower and remove the green leaves. Break the florets off the center core; cut the core into 1-inch cubes. Wash the cauliflower under cold running water.

2. In a 3- to 4-quart enameled or stainless-steel saucepan, bring 1 quart of water and the salt to a boil over high heat.

3. Drop in the cauliflower and cook briskly, uncovered, for 10 minutes, or until the pieces are tender but still somewhat resistant to the point of a small, sharp knife.

4. Drain in a sieve or colander.

5. In a heavy 10- to 12-inch skillet with a deep-frying thermometer or in an electric skillet, heat 1 or 2 inches of the oil or shortening until it reaches a temperature of 375°.

6. Pat the cauliflower completely dry with paper towels, and a dozen or so pieces at a time, fry them in the hot oil for about 15 minutes, or until golden brown on all sides. As they brown, remove them with a slotted spoon and drain them on paper towels.

7. They may be served hot or at room temperature. In either case, mound the cauliflower on a platter and spread the sesame sauce over it.

SESAME SAUCE

3 medium-sized garlic cloves, peeled and finely chopped
1 cup *tahina* paste (ground, hulled sesame seeds)
¾ to 1 cup cold water
½ cup fresh lemon juice
1 teaspoon salt

1. In a deep bowl, mash the garlic to a paste with a pestle or the back of a large spoon.
2. Stir in the *tahina*.
3. Then, with a whisk or spoon, beat in ½ cup of the cold water, the lemon juice, and salt. Still beating, add up to ½ cup more of water, 1 tablespoon at a time, until the sauce has the consistency of thick mayonnaise and holds its shape almost solidly in a spoon.
4. Taste for seasoning.

Cauliflower with Garlic Sauce

Coliflor al Ajo Arriero   *To serve 4 to 6*

A 1- to 1½-pound head of cauliflower, trimmed and separated into florets
Salt
Vegetable oil or shortening for deep frying
White pepper
½ cup flour
2 eggs, lightly beaten
¾ cup soft fresh crumbs made from French or Italian bread, trimmed of crusts and pulverized in a blender or pulled apart with a fork
6 tablespoons olive oil
2 garlic cloves, peeled and lightly bruised with the flat of a knife
1 tablespoon paprika
2 tablespoons white vinegar
3 tablespoons boiling water

1. Drop the cauliflower florets into enough lightly salted boiling water to cover them by at least 1 inch.

2. Cook briskly, uncovered, for 8 to 10 minutes, or until the cauliflower shows only the slightest resistance when pierced with the point of a small, sharp knife. Drain on paper towels.

3. Heat 3 to 4 inches of vegetable oil or shortening in a deep-fat fryer or large, heavy saucepan until it reaches 350° on a deep-frying thermometer.

4. Sprinkle the florets liberally with salt and a little white pepper, dip them in the flour and shake vigorously to remove the excess. Then dip them in the beaten eggs and into the crumbs.

5. Turning them with tongs, deep-fry the florets (in two batches, if necessary) for about 4 minutes, or until they are golden brown. Drain on paper towels.

6. Then arrange them on a heated platter and drape with foil to keep them warm.

Celery and Dried Shrimp

Hsia-mi-pan-ch' in-ts' ai   *To serve 4 to 6*

1 bunch celery
20 Chinese dried shrimp
1 tablespoon Chinese rice wine, or pale dry
    sherry
1 tablespoon warm water
1 teaspoon soy sauce
½ teaspoon salt
1 tablespoon sugar
1 tablespoon white vinegar
2 teaspoons sesame-seed oil

PREPARE AHEAD: 1. Wash the shrimp under cold running water. In a small bowl, combine them with the wine and 1 tablespoon of warm water. Let them marinate for 30 minutes. Drain, saving the marinade.
2. Remove and discard the leaves of the celery and any stringy stalks. Cut the stalks lengthwise in two, then crosswise into 1-inch pieces.

TO ASSEMBLE: 1. In a large glass bowl, combine the reserve shrimp marinade, soy sauce, salt, sugar, vinegar and sesame-seed oil, and stir until the sugar dissolves.
2. Add the shrimp and celery, and toss them about until they are coated with the dressing.
3. Chill for 1 hour before serving.

Celery Victor

                                    To serve 6

3 bunches celery, about 2 inches in
    diameter
1½ cups chicken stock, fresh or canned
An herb bouquet of 4 sprigs parsley, 1 bay
    leaf and celery leaves tied together
Salt
Freshly ground black pepper
3 tablespoons white-wine vinegar
½ cup olive oil
12 flat anchovy fillets
12 strips pimiento
6 slices tomato (optional)
6 slices hard-cooked eggs (optional)
1½ teaspoons finely chopped fresh parsley

1. Remove the outer stalks of the celery, leaving a heart about 1 inch wide and 6 inches long.
2. Cut each celery heart in half lengthwise. Cut away all but the small leaves and trim the root ends (do not cut too deep; the celery halves should hold together). Use the cutaway leaves for the herb bouquet.
3. With a sharp knife, scrape the outer stalks if they seem coarse.
4. Arrange the celery halves side by side in a 10- or 12-inch skillet, preferably enameled or stainless-steel, and pour in the stock, using more stock or water if the celery is not completely covered.
5. Add the herb bouquet, with as much salt and pepper as suits your taste, and bring to a boil.
6. Reduce the heat to its lowest point, cover tightly and simmer the celery for about 15 minutes, or until it shows no resistance when pierced with the tip of a sharp knife.
7. With tongs or a slotted spoon, transfer the celery halves to a deep platter that will hold them in a single layer.
8. With a whisk, beat the vinegar and the oil together and pour over the celery while it is still warm.
9. Refrigerate for at least an hour before serving.
10. To serve, arrange the celery halves on individual chilled plates and crisscross 2 anchovy fillets and 2 strips of pimiento over each serving. Or instead, if you prefer, garnish the celery with a slice of tomato and a slice of hard-cooked egg. In either case, moisten the celery with a spoonful or so of the vinegar-olive oil sauce and sprinkle with chopped parsley.

Corn Pancakes

Tortillas de Maíz   *To make 8 pancakes*

**1 cup fresh corn kernels cut from 2 large
  ears of corn, or substitute 1 cup
  thoroughly defrosted frozen corn kernels**
⅓ cup vegetable oil
8 eggs
2 tablespoons flour
1½ teaspoons salt
½ teaspoon freshly ground black pepper
4 to 6 tablespoons butter
½ cup sour cream
2 tablespoons finely chopped fresh parsley

1. With paper towels, pat the corn kernels completely dry. In a heavy 8- to 10-inch skillet, heat the oil over moderate heat until a light haze forms above it.
2. Drop in the corn and cook, stirring frequently, for 10 minutes, or until the corn is golden brown. Drain the corn on a double thickness of paper towels.
3. Make the pancake batter in a large bowl, beating the eggs until they are well combined and foamy, then beating in the flour, salt and pepper.
4. Melt 1 tablespoon of the butter in a heavy 5- to 6-inch skillet or crêpe pan set over moderate heat.
5. When the foam subsides, pour in ¼ cup of the batter. As soon as the edges begin to set, sprinkle the tortilla with 2 tablespoons of corn. Then with a fork, push the edges of the tortilla toward the center of the pan and tip it slightly to allow the uncooked batter to run out and cover the exposed areas of the pan.
6. When the tortilla is set and the bottom a light brown, turn it over with a spatula and cook for 1 minute to brown the other side.
7. Slide the tortilla onto a heated platter and proceed similarly with the remaining batter, stirring the batter before making each tortilla.
8. Add a teaspoon of the remaining butter to the pan for each one.
9. As they are done, stack the pancakes one on top of the other.
10. Serve them on individual plates, topped with a tablespoon of sour cream and a sprinkling of chopped fresh parsley.

Corn Oysters

To make about 20

**1 cup grated fresh corn (from 3 to 4
  medium-sized cobs)**
1 egg yolk, beaten
2 tablespoons flour
¼ teaspoon salt
Freshly ground black pepper
1 egg white
¼ to ½ cup vegetable shortening
Salt

1. In a small mixing bowl, combine the grated corn, egg yolk, flour, salt and a few grindings of black pepper.
2. With a whisk or rotary beater, beat the egg white until it forms unwavering peaks on the beater when it is lifted out of the bowl. Gently but thoroughly fold it into the corn mixture.
3. In an 8- to 10-inch heavy skillet, heat 2 tablespoons of shortening over high heat until a light haze forms over it.
4. Drop the batter by teaspoonfuls into the fat (the corn oysters should be about the size of silver dollars) and fry them for a minute or two on each side, watching them carefully for any sign of burning and regulating the heat accordingly.
5. Drain the corn oysters on paper towels, batch by batch as you proceed, and add more shortening to the pan as needed. There should be a thin film of fat on the bottom of the pan at all times.
6. Before serving on a heated platter, sprinkle the corn oysters liberally with salt. These make good accompaniments to meat and chicken dishes, or serve alone with maple syrup.

Puréed Corn with Scallions and Peppers

Humitas   *To serve 4 to 6*

**4 cups fresh corn kernels, cut from about 8
  large ears of corn, or substitute 4 cups
  thoroughly defrosted frozen corn kernels**
⅓ cup milk
2 eggs
2 teaspoons paprika
½ teaspoon salt
Freshly ground black pepper
¼ cup butter
½ cup coarsely chopped scallions
¼ cup coarsely chopped geen pepper
⅓ cup freshly grated Parmesan cheese

1. Combine the corn and milk in the jar of a blender and blend at high speed for 30 seconds.
2. Add the eggs, paprika, salt and a few grindings of black pepper and blend for 15 seconds longer, or until the mixture is thick and smooth.
3. To make the corn mixture by hand, purée the corn through a food mill set over a bowl. Discard the pulp left in the mill. Add the milk, eggs, paprika, salt and pepper, and mix vigorously with a spoon or whisk until the mixture is thick and smooth.)
4. In a heavy 10-inch skillet, melt the butter over moderate heat. When the foam subsides, add the scallions and green pepper, and cook, stirring, for 4 or 5 minutes, or until the vegetables are soft but not brown.
5. Pour in the corn mixture, reduce the heat, and simmer, uncovered, stirring frequently, for 5 to 7 minutes, or until the mixture thickens somewhat.
6. Stir in the grated cheese and, as soon as it melts, remove the skillet from the heat. Serve as accompaniment to meat dishes.

Cucumbers with Sour Cream and Dill

Schmorgurken mit saurem Rahm und Dill   *To serve 6*

**6 medium-sized firm, fresh cucumbers
  (about 3 pounds)**
2 teaspoons salt
2 tablespoons butter
½ cup finely chopped onions
2 tablespoons flour
2 cups milk
2 tablespoons sour cream
1 tablespoon finely chopped fresh parsley
**1 tablespoon finely chopped fresh dill, or
  substitute 1 teaspoon dried dill weed**

1. With a small, sharp knife, peel the cucumbers and cut them in half lengthwise. Seed them by running the tip of a small spoon down them, from end to end.
2. Cut the cucumber halves crosswise into 1-inch pieces and place them in a large bowl.
3. Sprinkle them with salt, tossing them about with a spoon to spread it evenly.
4. Let the cucumbers stand at room temperature for 30 minutes, then drain off all the liquid and pat them dry with paper towels.
5. In a heavy 10- to 12-inch skillet, melt the butter over moderate heat.
6. When the foam subsides, add the onions and cook, stirring frequently, for 8 to 10 minutes, or until they color lightly.
7. Add the flour and cook, stirring constantly, until the flour turns a golden brown. Watch for any sign of burning and regulate the heat accordingly.
8. Pour in the milk and, stirring constantly, bring to a boil.
9. Reduce the heat to low and simmer for 1 or 2 minutes, until the mixture thickens slightly.
10. Add the cucumbers and simmer, uncovered, for 15 minutes.
11. When the cucumbers are tender but not pulpy, add the sour cream, parsley and dill. Taste for seasoning.
12. Serve in a heated bowl.

Stuffed Cucumbers

Gefüllte Gurken   *To serve 6 to 8*

2 cucumbers, 6 to 8 inches long
½ teaspoon salt
2 boneless sardines
¼ pound boiled ham, diced
2 hard-cooked eggs, coarsely chopped
2 teaspoons finely chopped onions
2 tablespoons minced sour pickles
1 teaspoon Dijon-style mustard
2 to 4 tablespoons mayonnaise, freshly
made or a good commercial brand

1. Cut ½ inch off the tip of each cucumber, then peel the cucumbers with a vegetable scraper or sharp knife. Cut out the seeds and center pulp with a long iced-tea spoon, leaving a shell about ¼-inch thick.
2. Pour ¼ teaspoon of salt into each cucumber, rubbing it in evenly with your forefinger, let the shells stand about 15 minutes, then dry them inside with a piece of paper towel.
3. In a medium-sized mixing bowl, mash the sardines to a paste with a fork or wooden spoon.
4. Add the ham, eggs, onions, pickles, mustard and 2 tablespoons of mayonnaise. Stir the ingredients together until the mixture holds its shape in a spoon. (If it seems too dry, add more mayonnaise.) Taste for seasoning. The amount of salt needed will depend on the saltiness of the sardines and ham.
5. Stuff the cucumbers by standing them on end and spooning the filling in, tamping it down with a spoon as you proceed. When they are all tightly packed, wrap them separately in wax paper or aluminum foil and refrigerate them for 2 hours, or until the filling is firm.
6. To serve, slice the cucumbers crosswise, on a slant, in slices about ½ inch thick.

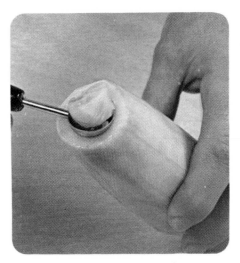

1. For stuffed cucumbers, peel one, cut off the end opposite the stem, scoop pulp and seeds from center.

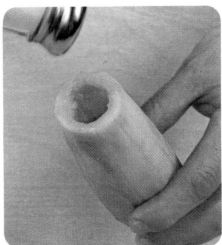

2. Shake ¼ teaspoon of salt down into the hollow core to draw out the cucumber's natural liquids.

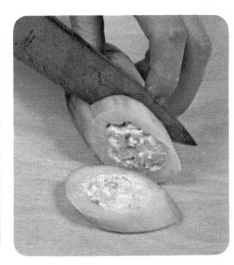

3. After cucumber has been stuffed with filling, refrigerate it for several hours. Then slice it on a slant.

Eggplant, tomatoes, green peppers, garlic cloves and a garnish of lemon are all used to make to Turkish dish, *kizarmiş patlican*, described below.

Eggplant with Green Peppers

Kizarmiş Patlican   *To serve 6*

2 tablespoons plus 1½ cups olive oil
4 medium-sized tomatoes, peeled, seeded and coarsely chopped
2 large garlic cloves, peeled and thinly sliced
1 teaspoon plus ¼ cup salt
A medium-sized eggplant (about 1 pound)
2 medium-sized green peppers, seeded, deribbed and cut lengthwise into quarters
1 lemon, cut in wedges

1. In a heavy 8- to 10-inch skillet, heat 2 tablespoons of the olive oil over moderate heat until a light haze forms above it.
2. Add the tomatoes, garlic and 1 teaspoon of the salt.
3. Mashing and stirring frequently, cook the tomatoes briskly until almost all their liquid evaporates and they become a thick, somewhat smooth purée. Set aside off the heat.
4. With a large, sharp knife, peel the eggplant and cut off the stem end. Cut the eggplant lengthwise into ½-inch-thick slices.
5. Then one a time lay each slice flat and cut lengthwise strips at ½-inch intervals starting at the wide end and cutting to within about 2 inches of the narrow end. The slices should now look like fans.
6. Combine 1 quart of water and the remain-ing ¼ cup of salt in a shallow bowl or baking dish, and add the eggplant sections. Turn them about to coat them evenly with the brine, and let them soak at room temperature for about 10 minutes to rid them of any bitterness.
7. In a heavy 12-inch skillet, heat the remain-ing 1½ cups of oil over high heat until a light haze forms above it.
8. Pat the eggplant completely dry with paper towels.
9. Regulating the heat so the eggplant colors evenly without burning, fry it 3 or 4 slices at a time for about 5 minutes on each side, or until it is lightly browned and shows no resistance when pierced with the tines of a fork.
10. Transfer the eggplant to paper towels and fry the remaining slices.
11. Add the green peppers to the oil remain-ing in the skillet, adding more oil if necessary.
12. Cook the peppers over moderate heat for about 10 minutes, turning them over with tongs. When they are soft but still somewhat firm to the touch, drain them on paper towels.
13. Peel off the skins with a small, sharp knife.
14. Mound the eggplant slices in the center of a serving platter and pour the tomato sauce over them.
15. Fold the peppers in half lengthwise and arrange them around the eggplant.
16. Serve at room temperature, garnished with lemon.

Eggplant with Tomatoes and Onions

Imam Bayildi   *To serve 6*

3 medium-sized eggplants (about 1 pound each), as long and narrow as possible

4 tablespoons plus 2 teaspoons salt

6 medium-sized onions, peeled, sliced ⅛ inch thick and separated into rings

5 medium-sized fresh, ripe tomatoes, peeled, seeded and finely chopped, or substitute 1½ cups chopped, drained, canned tomatoes

½ cup olive oil

6 large garlic cloves, peeled

1 cup water

2 tablespoons finely chopped parsley, preferably flat-leaf parsley

1. With a sharp knife, cut off the stem and peel each eggplant lengthwise, leaving 4 evenly spaced 1-inch-wide strips of peel intact. Slicing between the strips, cut each one in half.

2. Cut side up, make three or four 4-inch-long lengthwise slashes through the thickest part of each half, spacing the slashes about 1 inch apart.

3. Sprinkle the eggplants with 1 tablespoon of the salt and arrange them in two or three layers in a large flat bowl or pan.

4. Pour in enough cold water to cover them by 1 inch, weight with a heavy casserole, and let the eggplants rest at room temperature for at least 30 minutes.

Eggplant stuffed with onions and chopped tomatoes produced a Turkish delight called "the Imam fainted" – because a priest swooned when denied the dish.

5. Meanwhile, drop the onion rings into a large colander set in a deep plate.

6. Sprinkle the onions with 3 tablespoons of the salt, turning them about with a spoon to coat them evenly.

7. Let stand at room temperature for at least 30 minutes, then rinse the onions under warm running water and squeeze them gently but completely dry.

8. Place them in a bowl, add the tomatoes and the remaining 2 teaspoons of salt and toss together thoroughly.

9. Pour 2 tablespoons of the oil into a heavy casserole large enough to hold the eggplants in one layer.

10. Drain the eggplants, rinse them under cold water and pat dry with paper towels. Arrange the eggplants cut side up in the casserole.

11. Force as much of the onion-tomato mixture as possible into the slashes and spread the rest on top.

12. Place a garlic clove on each eggplant half, and sprinkle them with the remaining 6 tablespoons of oil. Pour in the cup of water and bring to a boil over high heat.

13. Reduce the heat to low and simmer covered for 1 hour and 15 minutes, or until the eggplants are tender.

14. Cool in the casserole to room temperature.

15. To serve, arrange the eggplants on a large platter or individual serving plates, spoon the cooking juices around them and sprinkle with parsley.

Eggplant with Cheese

Parmigiana di Melanzane   *To serve 4*

**1½ pounds eggplant, peeled and cut in
  ½-inch slices**
Salt
Flour
¼ to ½ cup olive oil
2 cups tomato sauce (page 64)
8 ounces *mozzarella* cheese, thinly sliced
**½ cup freshly grated imported Parmesan
  cheese**

1. Preheat the oven to 400°.
2. Choose a shallow 1½- to 2-quart baking dish that is attractive enough to serve from and rub it with oil.
3. Sprinkle both sides of the eggplant slices with salt (to draw out their moisture) and spread them out in one layer on a platter or board.
4. After 20 to 30 minutes, pat the eggplant dry with paper towels.
5. Dip each slice in flour and shake or brush off the excess.
6. In a heavy 10- to 12-inch skillet, heat ¼ cup of olive oil until a light haze forms over it and brown the eggplant slices a few at a time, working quickly to prevent them from soaking up too much oil. If the oil cooks away, add more.
7. As the eggplant browns, transfer the slices to fresh paper towels to drain.
8. Now pour ¼ inch of the tomato sauce into the oiled baking-and-serving dish.
9. Spread the drained eggplant slices over the sauce, top them with a layer of *mozzarella* cheese, and sprinkle over it part of the grated Parmesan cheese.
10. Repeat with 1 or 2 more layers (depending on the capacity of the baking dish), but be sure to finish up with layers of the tomato sauce, *mozzarella* and Parmesan.
11. Cover the dish snugly with foil and bake in the middle of the oven for 20 minutes.
12. Remove the foil and bake uncovered for 10 minutes longer.

Eggplant with Soy Sauce

To serve 8

1 large eggplant
¼ cup sesame or vegetable oil
3 tablespoons soy sauce
2 teaspoons sugar
¼ cup beef or chicken broth
½ teaspoon MSG

1. Peel the eggplant and cut as for French fried potatoes.
2. Heat the oil in a skillet; add the eggplant and cook until it is lightly browned on all sides.
3. Add a mixture of the soy sauce, sugar, broth and MSG.
4. Cook over low heat for 10 minutes.
5. Serve hot.

Cold Eggplant Purée

To make about 2 cups

1 medium-sized eggplant (about 1 pound)
¼ cup fresh lemon juice
2 tablespoons sesame sauce (*page 17*)
1 large garlic clove, peeled and finely
  chopped
1 teaspoon salt
1 tablespoon olive oil
¼ cup finely chopped onions
1 tablespoon finely chopped parsley,
  preferably flat-leaf parsley

1. First, roast the eggplant in the following fashion: Prick it in 3 or 4 places with the tines of a long-handled fork, then impale it on the fork and turn it over a gas flame until the skin chars and begins to crack. (Or, if you have an electric stove, pierce the eggplant, place it on a baking sheet and broil 4 inches from the heat for about 20 minutes, turning it to char on all sides.)
2. When the eggplant is cool enough to handle, peel it, cutting away any badly charred spots on the flesh. Cut the eggplant in half lengthwise and chop it finely.
3. Then mash the pulp to a smooth purée, beat in the lemon juice, sesame sauce, garlic and salt. Taste for seasoning.
4. To serve, spread the purée on a serving plate or mound it in a bowl and sprinkle the top with the olive oil, chopped onions and parsley.

Spiced Eggplant with Yoghurt

Baingan ka Rayta   *To serve 4 to 6*

1 medium-sized eggplant (about 1 pound)
2 tablespoons vegetable oil
¼ cup finely chopped onions
1 teaspoon salt
1 tablespoon *garam masala* (page 35)
1 small firm, ripe tomato, coarsely
  chopped
¼ cup finely chopped fresh coriander
1 cup unflavored yoghurt

1. Preheat the oven to 400°
2. With the point of a sharp knife, make 5 or 6 inch-deep evenly spaced slits in the eggplant and place it in a shallow baking dish.
3. Roast the eggplant in the middle of the oven for 45 minutes, or until it is soft to the touch. Watch carefully for any signs of burning and regulate the heat accordingly.
4. Remove the eggplant from the oven and when it is cool enough to handle, peel it and chop the pulp coarsely.
5. Meanwhile, in a heavy 8- to 10-inch skillet, heat the vegetable oil over moderate heat until a light haze forms above it.
6. Add the onions and salt and, stirring constantly, cook for 7 or 8 minutes, or until they are soft and golden brown. Watch carefully for any signs of burning, and regulate the heat accordingly.
7. Add the *garam masala,* tomato and coriander, and stir for 1 minute. Still stirring, add the eggplant, and cook for 2 or 3 minutes longer.
8. Place the yoghurt in a small bowl, add the entire contents of the skillet, and gently but thoroughly toss the ingredients together.
9. Taste for seasoning, cover tightly, and refrigerate for at least 1 hour, or until completely chilled.

Eggplant, Tomato and Chick-Pea Casserole

Musakka'a   *To serve 6*

1½ cups dried chick-peas, or substitute 2
  cups drained, canned chick-peas
Olive oil
2 medium-sized eggplants, about 1 pound
  each, washed but not peeled, and cut
  into 2-inch cubes
3 medium-sized onions, peeled and cut
  into ¼-inch-thick slices

3 teaspoons salt
Freshly ground black pepper
12 medium-sized fresh, ripe tomatoes, peeled, seeded and finely chopped, or substitute
  4 cups chopped, drained, canned tomatoes
1½ cups water

NOTE: Starting a day ahead, wash the dried
chick-peas in a sieve under cold running
water, then place them in a large bowl or pan
and add enough cold water to cover them

This meatless *musakka'a*, made with chick peas, eggplants, onions and tomatoes,
must be planned a day ahead in order to give the chick-peas time to soak.

by 2 inches. Soak at room temperature for at least 12 hours.

1. Drain the peas and place them in a heavy 2- to 3-quart saucepan.
2. Add enough fresh water to the chick-peas to cover them completely and bring to a boil over high heat.
3. Reduce the heat to low and simmer partially covered for about 2 to 2½ hours until the peas are tender but still intact. Replenish with more boiling water from time to time if necessary.
4. Drain the peas in a sieve or colander. (Canned chick-peas require no cooking and need only to be drained and rinsed thoroughly under cold running water.)
5. Preheat the oven to 400°.
6. In a heavy 12-inch skillet, heat about 1 inch of oil over high heat almost to the smoking point.
7. Drop in the eggplant cubes and, stirring frequently, cook for about 5 minutes, or until they are lightly browned on all sides.
8. With a slotted spoon, transfer them to a 9-by-14-by-2½-inch baking-serving dish and spread them out evenly.
9. Add the onions to the oil remaining in the skillet and, stirring frequently, cook over moderate heat for 8 to 10 minutes, or until they are soft and delicately browned. Watch carefully for any signs of burning and regulate the heat accordingly.
10. Spread the onions and all of their cooking oil on top of the eggplant and pour over them an additional ½ cup of olive oil.
11. Sprinkle the onions with 1 teaspoon of the salt and a few grindings of pepper.
12. Scatter the chick-peas on top, and cover them with the tomatoes.
13. Sprinkle with the remaining 2 teaspoons of salt and a few grindings of pepper and pour in the water.
14. Bring the *musakka'a* to a boil on top of the stove, then bake in the lower third of the

oven for 40 minutes, or until the vegetables are very tender.
15. Cool to room temperature and serve directly from the baking dish.

Kale in Cream Sauce

Grønlangkaal   *To serve 6 to 8*

1 pound kale
2 teaspoons salt
4 tablespoons butter
4 tablespoons flour
1 cup milk
1 cup heavy cream
½ teaspoon freshly ground black pepper

1. Discard any tough large leaves of the kale, remove any tough stems and wash the leaves carefully under cold running water, shaking to remove any sand. Shake the kale again to remove excess water, and tear it into large pieces.
2. Place the kale in a 4- to 6-quart saucepan with ½ teaspoon of the salt and just enough cold water to barely cover it.
3. Cook, tightly covered, over medium heat for about 15 minutes, or until the kale is very tender (test by tasting a leaf).
4. Drain the kale through a sieve, pressing down on the vegetable with a large spoon to extract all of the moisture. Then chop very fine.
5. In a heavy 2- to 3-quart saucepan, prepare the following sauce: Melt the butter over medium heat; remove the pan from the heat and stir in the flour. Add the milk and cream all at once, beating vigorously with a wire whisk. Return the pan to low heat and cook, whisking constantly, until the sauce comes to a boil and is smooth and thick.
6. Add the remaining salt, pepper and the chopped kale, taste for seasoning if necessary and cook for another 1 or 2 minutes, or until the kale is heated through.

Braised Leeks with Rice

Zeytinyagli Pirasa   *To serve 4 to 6*

**2 pounds firm, fresh leeks, each approx-
  imately 1½ inches in diameter**
¼ cup olive oil
1 cup finely chopped onions
1 teaspoon flour
1 teaspoon salt
½ teaspoon sugar
1½ cups water
**3 tablespoons uncooked long- or medium-
  grain white rice**
**2 lemons, each cut lengthwise into 6 or 8
  wedges**

1. With a sharp knife, cut the roots from the leeks. Strip away any withered leaves and cut off and discard all but about 2 inches of the green tops.
2. Then wash the leeks under cold running water, spreading the leaves apart to rid them of sand.
3. Slice the leeks crosswise into 1-inch lengths, and set aside.
4. In a heavy 3- to 4-quart casserole, heat the oil over moderate heat until a light haze forms above it.
5. Add the onions and, stirring frequently, cook for 5 minutes, or until they are limp and transparent but not brown.
6. Stir in the flour, salt and sugar, cook for a minute or so, then add the water and raise the heat to high. Stirring constantly, cook briskly until the mixture comes to a boil and thickens slightly.
7. Add the rice and leeks, turning them about with a spoon to coat them evenly with sauce.
8. Reduce the heat to low, cover tightly and simmer for 30 minutes, or until the leeks and rice are tender but still intact. Taste for seasoning.
9. Cool to room temperature and serve directly from the casserole, accompanied by the lemon wedges.

Mushrooms and Onions in Sour Cream

To serve 4 to 6

4 tablespoons butter
2 medium onions, thinly sliced
**1 pound fresh mushrooms, 1 to 1½ inches
  in diameter**
1 cup sour cream
1 teaspoon lemon juice
1 teaspoon salt
Freshly ground black pepper
2 teaspoons finely chopped fresh parsley

1. In a heavy 10-inch skillet, melt the butter over medium heat. When the foam subsides, add the onions and cook for 6 to 8 minutes until the are lightly colored.
2. Stir in the mushrooms, cover the pan and cook, still over moderate heat, for about 7 minutes.
3. Add the sour cream, lemon juice, salt and a few grindings of pepper; simmer, stirring, until the cream is heated through. Don't let it boil.
4. Taste for seasoning and sprinkle with chopped parsley.

Mushrooms with Tomatoes and Bacon

Pilze mit Tomaten und Speck   *To serve 4*

1 pound fresh mushrooms
2 tablespoons butter
½ cup finely diced lean bacon
½ cup finely chopped onions
½ teaspoon salt
Freshly ground black pepper
**3 medium-sized tomatoes, peeled, seeded
  and coarsely chopped**
2 tablespoons finely chopped fresh parsley

1. Cut away any tough ends of the mushrooms stems. Wipe the mushrooms with a damp paper towel, and cut them, stems and all, into ⅛-inch slices.

2. In a heavy 10- to 12-inch skillet, melt the butter over moderate heat. When the foam subsides, add the bacon and cook, stirring frequently, until the bacon is crisp and light brown.

3. Add the onions and cook, stirring frequently, for 5 minutes, or until the onions are soft and transparent but not brown.

4. Then drop in the mushrooms and season with salt and a few grindings of pepper.

5. Cook over high heat, turning the mushrooms frequently, for 3 or 4 minutes.

6. When the mushrooms are lightly colored, stir in the chopped tomatoes and simmer over low heat for about 10 minutes.

7. If there are more than 2 or 3 tablespoons of liquid left in the pan, increase the heat and boil briskly for a minute or so to reduce the excess. Then add the parsley and taste for seasoning.

8. Serve at once from a heated bowl.

1. In a heavy 10- to 12-inch stainless-steel or enameled skillet, melt 4 tablespoons of butter over moderate heat. When the foam subsides, add the chopped onions and cook 3 to 5 minutes, or until the onions are soft and transparent but not brown.

2. Now add the mushroom slices and cook another 3 to 5 minutes. Shake the pan from time to time so that the mushrooms do not stick.

3. When the mushrooms are a light, delicate brown, sprinkle in the bread crumbs and toss the contents of the pan gently with a rubber spatula or wooden spoon.

4. Remove the pan from the heat.

5. In a small bowl, beat the sour cream with a wooden spoon or whisk for a minute or two, then stir it into the skillet. Toss lightly until the mushrooms are well coated with the cream.

Sliced Mushrooms in Sour Cream

Paistetut Sienet   *To serve 4*

4 tablespoons butter
¼ cup finely chopped onions
1 pound fresh mushrooms, thinly sliced
¼ cup dry bread crumbs
½ cup sour cream

Okra and Tomatoes

To serve 8

2 tablespoons vegetable oil
1 cup chopped onions
1½ cups chopped tomatoes
½ teaspoon cumin
3 packages frozen okra or 2 cans, drained
1¼ teaspoon salt

1. Heat the oil in a skillet, then sauté the onions until they are golden brown.

2. Add the tomatoes and cumin, bring to a boil, then add the okra and salt.

3. Cover and cook over low heat for 20 minutes, or until the okra is tender.

French Fried Onion Rings

To serve 4 to 6

3 egg yolks
1½ cups flour
½ teaspoon baking soda
1½ teaspoons salt
2 cups buttermilk
Vegetable oil or shortening for deep frying
4 large yellow onions, 3 to 4 inches in diameter, peeled and cut in ¼-inch-thick slices
Salt

1. In a mixing bowl, combine the egg yolks, flour, baking soda and salt, and beat them together with a large spoon.
2. Pour in the buttermilk slowly, beating until the mixture forms a fairly smooth paste.
3. Heat the shortening in a deep-fat fryer – the fat should be at least 3 inches deep – until it registers 375° on a deep-fat thermometer.
4. Separate the onion slices into rings, drop them in the batter and then, 7 or 8 rings at a time, fry them in the fat for 4 to 5 minutes until lightly browned.
5. Transfer them to paper towels while you proceed with the next batch.
6. When all the onion rings are done, fry them again in the hot fat for a minute or two to heat them through and crisp them.
7. Drain on paper towels and serve sprinkled with salt.

Creamed Onions and Peas

To serve 8

24 to 28 peeled white onions, about 1 inch in diameter
3 cups fresh green peas (about 3 pounds), or 3 packages frozen green peas, thoroughly defrosted
4 tablespoons butter
4 tablespoons flour
1½ cups milk
½ cup cream
1 teaspoon salt
Pinch of white pepper
¼ teaspoon nutmeg

1. Place the onions in a 3- or 4-quart saucepan with enough water to cover them by about an inch. Salt the water lightly.
2. Bring to a boil, then reduce the heat to its lowest point and simmer the onions partially covered for about 20 minutes, or until they show only the slightest resistance when pierced with the tip of a small, sharp knife.
3. Drain the onions in a sieve set over a small bowl and set aside. Reserve the cooking water to use in making the sauce.
4. Cook the fresh peas by dropping them into 6 or 7 quarts of rapidly boiling salted water. Boil them briskly uncovered for 8 to 10 minutes, or until they are tender.
5. Then drain the peas and immerse them in a bowl of cold water for 2 or 3 minutes. This will stop their cooking and help keep their bright green color.
6. Drain again and put the peas aside with the cooked onions. Frozen peas need not be cooked, merely defrosted.
7. In a heavy 3-quart saucepan, melt the butter over moderate heat and stir in the flour.
8. Remove the pan from the heat and pour in the 2 cups of the reserved onion-cooking liquid, beating with a wire whisk until the flour-butter mixture is partially dissolved.
9. Add the milk and cream, return the pan to the heat and cook, whisking constantly, until the sauce is smooth and thick.
10. Simmer for 3 to 4 minutes to remove any taste of uncooked flour, season with the salt, white pepper and nutmeg, then add the cooked onions and the cooked fresh peas or thoroughly defrosted frozen peas.
11. Simmer for 5 minutes, or until the vegetables are heated through.
12. Taste for seasoning and serve.

Spiced Peas with Homemade Cheese

Mattar Pannir   *To serve 4 to 6*

CHEESE
2 quarts milk
½ cup unflavored yoghurt
2 tablespoons fresh strained lemon juice
PEAS
5 tablespoons clarified butter
2 tablespoons scraped, finely chopped fresh ginger root
1 tablespoon finely chopped garlic
1 cup finely chopped onions
1 teaspoon salt
1 teaspoon turmeric
¼ teaspoon ground hot red pepper
1 teaspoon ground coriander
1 tablespoon *garam masala (below)*
2 cups finely chopped fresh tomatoes
1½ cups fresh green peas (about 1½ pounds unshelled) or 1 ten-ounce package frozen peas, thoroughly defrosted
1 teaspoon sugar (optional)
3 tablespoons finely chopped fresh coriander

1. Prepare the cheese in the following fashion: In a heavy 3- to 4-quart saucepan, bring the milk to a boil over high heat.

2. As soon as the foam begins to rise, remove the pan from the heat and gently but thoroughly stir in the yoghurt and lemon juice. The curds will begin to solidify immediately and separate from the liquid whey.

3. Pour the entire contents of the pan into a large sieve set over a bowl and lined with a double thickness of cheesecloth.

4. Let the curds drain undisturbed until the cloth is cool enough to handle. Then wrap the cloth tightly around the curds and wring it vigorously to squeeze out all the excess liquid.

5. Reserve 1 cup of the whey in the bowl and discard the rest.

6. Place the cheese, still wrapped in cheesecloth, on a cutting board and set another board or large flat-bottomed skillet on top of it. Weight the top with canned foods, flatirons, heavy pots or the like, weighing in all about 15 pounds, and let it rest in this fashion at room temperature for 6 to 8 hours, or until the cheese is firm and compact.

7. Unwrap the cheese, cut it into ½-inch cubes, cover with wax paper or plastic wrap, and refrigerate until ready to use. (There should be about 1 to 1½ cups of cheese cubes.)

8. To prepare the cheese and peas, heat the clarified butter in a heavy 10- to 12-inch skillet until a drop of water flicked into it splutters instantly.

9. Add the cheese cubes and fry them for 4 to 5 minutes, turning the cubes about gently but constantly with a slotted spoon until they are golden brown on all sides. As they brown, transfer the cubes of cheese to a plate.

10. Add the ginger and garlic to the butter remaining in the skillet and, stirring constantly, fry for 30 seconds.

11. Add the onions and salt and, stirring occasionally, continue to fry for 7 or 8 minutes, or until the onions are soft and golden brown. Watch carefully for any signs of burning and regulate the heat accordingly.

12. Stir in ¼ cup of the reserved whey, then add the turmeric, red pepper, ground coriander and *garam masala.* When they are well blended, stir in the remaining ¾ cup of whey and the tomatoes, and bring to a boil over high heat.

13. Reduce the heat to low and simmer partially covered for 10 minutes, stirring occasionally.

14. Add the peas and taste for seasoning. If the gravy has too acid a flavor add up to 1 teaspoon sugar.

15. Remove the cover and, stirring occasionally, cook for 3 minutes.

16. Then add the cheese cubes and 1 tablespoon of the fresh coriander, cover the skillet tightly, and simmmer over low heat for 10

Fresh garden peas and cubes of white homemade cheese are lavished with spices in this vegetarian dish from India. The recipe begins on page 33

to 20 minutes, or longer if you are using fresh peas and they are not yet tender.

17. To serve, transfer the entire contents of the pan to a heated bowl or deep platter and garnish the top with the remaining 2 tablespoons of chopped fresh coriander.

GARAM MASALA
To make about 1½ cups
5 three-inch pieces cinnamon stick
1 cup whole cardamom pods, preferably green cardamoms
½ cup whole cloves
½ cup whole cumin seeds
¼ cup whole coriander seeds
½ cup whole black peppercorns

1. Preheat the oven to 200°.
2. Spread the cinnamon, cloves, cumin, coriander and peppercorns in one layer in a large shallow roasting pan.
3. Roast on the bottom shelf of the oven for 30 minutes, stirring and turning the mixture two or three times with a large spoon. Do not let the spices brown.
4. Break open the cardamom pods between your fingers or place them one at a time on a flat surface and press down on the pod wth the ball of your thumb to snap it open.
5. Pull the pod away from the seeds inside and discard it. Set the seeds aside.
6. Place the roasted cinnamon sticks between the two layers of a folded linen towel and pound them with a rolling pin or a kitchen mallet until they are finely crushed.
7. Combine the cardamom seeds, crushed cinnamon, cloves, cumin seeds, coriander seeds and peppercorns in a small pan or bowl and stir them together until they are well mixed.
8. Grind the spices a cup or so at a time by pouring them into the jar of an electric blender and blending at high speed for 2 or 3 minutes, until they are completely pulverized and become a smooth powder. If the machine clogs and stops, turn it off, stir the spices once or twice, then continue blending.
9. As each cupful of spices is ground, transfer it to a jar or bottle with a tightly fitting lid.
10. *Garam masala* may be stored at room temperature in an airtight container, and will retain its full flavor for 5 or 6 months.

Braised Peas with Prosciutto

Piselli al Prosciutto   *To serve 4*

4 tablespoons butter
¼ cup finely chopped onions
2 cups fresh green peas (about 2 pounds unshelled)
¼ cup chicken stock, fresh or canned
2 ounces prosciutto, cut in 1-by-¼-inch julienne strips (about ¼ cup)
Salt
Freshly ground black pepper

1. In a heavy 1- to 2-quart saucepan, melt the 2 tablespoons of butter over moderate heat and cook the finely chopped onions for 7 or 8 minutes, stirring frequently until they are soft but not brown.
2. Stir in the green peas and chicken stock, cover, and cook for 15 to 20 minutes.
3. When the peas are tender, add the strips of prosciutto and cook, uncovered, stirring frequently, for 2 minutes more, or until all the liquid is absorbed. Taste for seasoning.
4. Serve the peas in a heated bowl.

Snow Peas with Mushrooms and Bamboo Shoots

Chao-hsüeh-tou   To serve 4

6 dried Chinese mushrooms, 1 to 1½ inches in diameter
1 pound fresh snow peas (thoroughly defrosted frozen snow peas will do, but they will not have the crispness of the fresh ones)
½ cup canned bamboo shoots, sliced ⅛ inch thick and cut into 1-by-1-inch triangular tree-shaped pieces
1½ teaspoons salt
½ teaspoon sugar
2 tablespoons peanut oil, or flavorless vegetable oil

PREPARE AHEAD: 1. In a small bowl, cover the mushrooms with ½ cup of warm water and let them soak for 30 minutes. Remove them with a slotted spoon. With a cleaver or sharp knife, cut away and discard the tough stems of the mushrooms and cut each cap into quarters. Strain the soaking water through a fine sieve and reserve 2 tablespoons of it.
2. Snap off the tips of the fresh snow peas and remove the strings from the pea pods.
3. Have the above ingredients, and the oil, bamboo shoots, salt and sugar within easy reach.

TO COOK: 1. Set a 12-inch wok or 10-inch skillet over high heat for 30 seconds.
2. Pour in the 2 tablespoons of oil, swirl it about in the pan and heat for another 30 seconds, turning the heat down to moderate if the oil begins to smoke. Immediately drop in the mushrooms and bamboo shoots, and stir-fry for 2 minutes.
3. Add the snow peas, salt and sugar, and then 2 tablespoons of the reserved mushroom-soaking water.
4. Cook, stirring constantly at high heat, for about 2 minutes, or until the water evaporates.
5. Transfer the contents of the pan to a heated platter and serve at once.

Fresh Peas with Onions and Lettuce

Petits Pois Frais à la Française   To serve 4 to 6

1 firm 7- to 8-inch Boston lettuce
3 cups fresh shelled green peas (about 3 pounds)
12 peeled white onions, about ¾ inch in diameter
6 parsley sprigs, tied together
6 tablespoons butter, cut into ½-inch pieces
½ cup water
½ teaspoon sugar
2 tablespoons soft butter

1. Remove the wilted outer leaves of the lettuce and trim the stem. Rinse the lettuce in cold water, spreading the leaves apart gently, to remove all traces of sand.
2. Cut the lettuce into 4 or 6 wedges, and bind each wedge with soft string to keep in shape while cooking.
3. In a heavy 3-quart saucepan, bring the peas, lettuce wedges, onions, parsley, 6 tablespoons butter, water, salt and sugar to a boil over moderate heat, toss lightly to mix flavors, then cover the pan tightly and cook for 30 minutes, stirring occasionally, until the peas and onions are tender and the liquid nearly cooked away. If the liquid hasn't evaporated, cook the peas uncovered, shaking the pan constantly, for a minute or two until it does.
4. Remove the parsley and cut the strings off the lettuce.
5. Gently stir in 2 tablespoons of soft butter; taste and season.
6. Transfer to a heated vegetable dish and serve in small bowls.

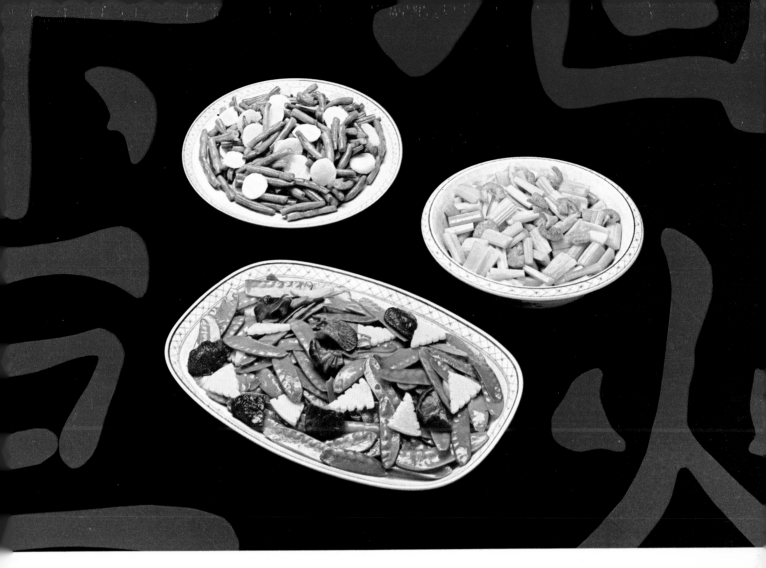

These Chinese dishes are, from top, string beans with water chestnuts *(below)*, celery and dried shrimp *(page 18)* and snow peas with mushrooms *(page 36)*.

String Beans with Water Chestnuts

Chao-ssu-chi-tou   *To serve 4*

1 pound fresh string beans
2 tablespoons peanut oil, or flavorless
   vegetable oil
1½ teaspoons salt
1 teaspoon sugar
10 water chestnuts, cut into ¼-inch slices
¼ cup chicken stock, fresh or canned
1 teaspon cornstarch dissolved in 1 tablespoon chicken stock, fresh or canned

PREPARE AHEAD: 1. Snap off and discard the ends of the beans, and, with a small knife,

remove any strings. Cut the beans into 2-inch pieces.
2. Have the beans, oil, salt, sugar, water chestnuts, chicken stock and cornstarch mixture within easy reach.

TO COOK: 1. Set a 12-inch wok or 10-inch skillet over high heat for 30 seconds.
2. Pour in the 2 tablespoons of oil, swirl it about in the pan and heat for another 30 seconds, turning the heat down to moderate if the oil begins to smoke.
3. Drop in the string beans and stir-fry for 3 minutes.
4. Add the salt, sugar and water chestnuts,

(continued on next page)

and stir once or twice before pouring in the stock.

5. Cover the pan and cook over moderate heat for 2 to 3 minutes until the beans are tender but still crisp.

6. Now give the cornstarch mixture a stir to recombine it and add it to the pan.

7. Cook, stirring, until the vegetables are coated with a light, clear glaze.

8. Transfer the entire contents of the pan to a heated platter and serve at once.

Italian Stuffed Peppers

Peperoni Imbottiti   *To serve 8*

Olive oil
4 tablespoons butter
3 cups fresh white bread crumbs
   (preferably French or Italian bread)
2 teaspoons finely chopped garlic
1 two-ounce can flat anchovy fillets,
   rinsed in cold water, dried and finely
   chopped
6 tablespoons capers, rinsed in cold water
   and finely chopped
8 black olives (preferably Mediterranean
   style), stoned and finely chopped
4 tablespoons finely chopped parsley,
   preferably the flat-leaf Italian type
Salt
Freshly ground black pepper
4 large green peppers, cut in half
   lengthwise, piths and seeds removed

1. Preheat the oven to 400°.

2. Pour 2 tablespoons of olive oil into a shallow baking dish large enough to hold the green pepper halves comfortably. Tip the dish back and forth to spread the oil evenly across the bottom.

3. In a heavy 8- to 10-inch skillet, melt the butter over moderate heat.

4. When the foam subsides, add the bread crumbs and cook them, stirring constantly, until they are crisp and lightly browned.

5. Remove the skillet from the heat and stir in the garlic.

6. Then add the anchovies, capers, black olives and parsley and mix well. Taste and season with salt and pepper. If the stuffing mixture looks too dry and crumbly, moisten it with a little olive oil.

7. Spoon the stuffing into the pepper halves and arrange them in the oiled baking dish.

8. Dribble a few drops of oil over the top of each pepper.

9. Bake in the middle of the oven for about 30 minutes, or until the peppers are tender but not limp and the stuffing is lightly browned on top.

10. Serve hot or cold

Fried Green Peppers

To serve 8

3 green peppers
Flour
1 egg, beaten
Cornstarch
Oil for deep frying

1. Wash and dry the peppers. Cut each pepper lengthwise into 8 pieces, discarding the seeds.

2. Dip the pepper strips in flour, then in the egg and finally in the cornstarch.

3. Heat the oil to 365° and fry the peppers until they are delicately browned.

4. Drain and serve hot.

Stuffed Peppers

To serve 6

6 green peppers
¾ sautéed chopped onions
1 cup sautéed sliced mushrooms
1½ cups cooked rice
Salt
Pepper
½ cup grated Parmesan cheese
2 tablespoons butter

1. Preheat the oven to 325°.
2. Put the peppers in a pan with cold water to cover. Bring slowly to a boil, then drain.
3. Cut off the tops of the peppers and scoop out the seeds.
4. Blend together the sautéed chopped onion, the sautéed sliced mushrooms, the cooked rice, salt and pepper.
5. Fill the peppers with this mixture, sprinkle them with the cheese, and dot with the butter.
6. Bake for 15 to 20 minutes.

Sweet Peppers with Tomatoes and Onions

Peperonata   *To serve 6*

2 tablespoons butter
¼ cup olive oil
1 pound onions, sliced ⅛ inch thick (about 4 cups)
2 pounds green and red peppers, peeled by blanching first, seeded and cut in 1-by-½-inch strips (about 6 cups)
2 pounds tomatoes, peeled, seeded and coarsely chopped (about 3 cups)
1 teaspoon red wine vinegar
1 teaspoon salt
Freshly ground black pepper

1. In a heavy 12-inch skillet, melt the 2 tablespoons of butter with the ¼ cup of olive oil over moderate heat.
2. Add the onions and cook them, turning them frequently, for 10 minutes, or until they are soft and lightly browned.
3. Stir in the peppers, reduce the heat, cover the skillet and cook for 10 minutes.
4. Add the tomatoes, vinegar, salt and a few grindings of black pepper; cover and cook for another 5 minutes.
5. Then cook the vegetables uncovered over high heat, stirring gently, until almost all the liquid has boiled away.
6. Serve the *peperonata* as a hot vegetable dish preceding or along with the main course, or refrigerate it and serve it cold as part of an *antipasto* or as an accompaniment to cold roast meats or fowl.

Potatoes in Parsley Sauce

Patatas en Salsa Verde   *To serve 4 to 6*

5 tablespoons olive oil
6 small boiling potatoes (about 2 pounds), peeled and sliced crosswise into ½-inch rounds
½ cup finely chopped onions
1 teaspoon finely chopped garlic
2 tablespoons finely chopped parsley
1 teaspoon salt
¼ teaspoon freshly ground black pepper
1½ cups boiling water

1. In a heavy 10- to 12-inch skillet, heat the olive oil over high heat until a light haze forms above it.
2. Add the potatoes. Turning them frequently with a metal spatula, cook for 10 minutes, or until they are a light golden brown on all sides.
3. Scatter the onions, garlic, parsley, salt and pepper on top of the potatoes and pour in the boiling water. Do not stir. Instead, shake the pan back and forth for a minute or two to distribute the water evenly.
4. Cover the skillet tightly and simmer over low heat for about 20 minutes, or until the potatoes are tender but not falling apart.
5. Shake the skillet back and forth occasionally to prevent the potatoes from sticking to the pan.
6. With a slotted spatula transfer the potatoes to a platter and pour a few teaspoonfuls of their cooking liquid over them.
7. Serve the remaining liquid separately in a sauceboat.

Butter-steamed New Potatoes

Sørdampete Nypoteter   To serve 4 to 6

20 to 24 tiny new potatoes (about 1 inch in diameter)
8 tablespoons (1 quarter-pound stick) unsalted butter
1 teaspoon salt
⅛ teaspoon white pepper
3 tablespoons finely chopped fresh dill

1. Scrub the potatoes under cold running water; then pat them thoroughly dry with paper towels.
2. Melt the ¼ pound of butter in a heavy, 6-quart casserole equipped with a cover.
3. Add the potatoes and sprinkle them with salt and pepper. Then coat them thoroughly with the melted butter by rolling them about in the casserole.
4. To ensure the success of this dish, the cover must fit the casserole tightly; if you have doubts, cover the casserole with a double thickness of aluminum foil, and pinch down the edges to seal it before putting on the lid.
5. Cook over low heat (an asbestos pad under the pan ensures against scorching) for 30 to 45 minutes, depending on the size of the potatoes.
6. Shake the casserole from time to time to prevent the potatoes from sticking.
7. When the potatoes can be easily pierced with the tip of a sharp knife, they are done.
8. Arrange them on a heated serving plate, sprinkle them with the chopped dill, and serve at once.

Spring Potatoes

To serve 6

2 pounds small new potatoes
3 cups water
2 teaspoons salt
3 tablespoons butter
2 tablespoons minced parsley

1. Peel the potatoes.
2. Bring the water and salt to a boil, then add the potatoes and cook them for 12 minutes, or until they are tender but slightly firm.
3. Drain the potatoes, return them to the saucepan and shake the pan over low heat until the potatoes are dry.
4. Add the butter and parsley. Toss until the butter melts and the potatoes are evenly coated.

Creamed Potatoes

To serve 8

3 pounds medium-sized potatoes
2 cups light cream
1 teaspoon salt
¼ teaspoon white pepper
⅛ teaspoon nutmeg
2 tablespoons butter
2 tablespoons minced parsley

1. Wash the unpeeled potatoes and cook them in boiling salted water for about 18 minutes, or until they are tender but still firm. Drain.
2. When the potatoes are cool enough to handle, peel them and cut in ¼-inch slices.
3. Put the potato slices, cream, salt, pepper and nutmeg in a skillet and cook over high heat until the cream is reduced to half.
4. Break the butter into small pieces and add it to the potatoes, swirling it in gently.
5. Taste for seasoning, sprinkle with the parsley and serve.

In Denmark caramelized potatoes are a Christmas specialty, but they can be enjoyed at any time of year. They are made by coating new potatoes with sugar.

Caramel Potatoes

Brunede Kartofler   *To serve 8*

24 small new potatoes
½ cup sugar
8 tablespoons (1 quarter-pound stick)
**   unsalted butter, melted**

1. Drop the unpeeled potatoes into a pan of boiling water and cook 15 to 20 minutes, or until they offer no resistance when pierced with the tip of a sharp knife.
2. Let them cool slightly; then peel them.
3. Melt the ½ cup of sugar in a heavy 10- to 12-inch skillet over low heat.

4. Cook slowly for 3 to 5 minutes, until the sugar turns to a light-brown caramel. Stir constantly with a wooden spoon and watch the sugar closely; the syrup changes color very rapidly and burns easily. It must not become too dark or it will be bitter.
5. Stir in the melted butter, and add as many potatoes as possible without crowding the pan.
6. Shake the pan almost constantly to roll the potatoes and coat them on all sides with the caramel.
7. Remove the hot, caramelized potatoes to a heated serving bowl and repeat the procedure until all the potatoes are coated.

Potatoes with Cabbage and Scallions

Colcannon   *To serve 4 to 6*

6 medium-sized boiling potatoes (about 2 pounds), peeled and quartered
4 cups finely shredded green cabbage (about 1 pound)
4 tablespoons butter
1 cup lukewarm milk
6 medium-sized scallions, including 2 inches of the green tops, cut lengthwise in half and crosswise into 1/8-inch slices
1 teaspoon salt
Freshly ground black pepper
1 tablespoon finely chopped fresh parsley

1. Drop the quartered potatoes into enough lightly salted boiling water to cover them by 2 inches, and boil briskly until they are tender but not falling apart.
2. Meanwhile, place the cabbage in a separate pot, pour in enough water to cover it completely, and bring to a boil. Boil rapidly, uncovered, for 10 minutes, then drain thoroughly in a colander.
3. Melt 2 tablespoons of the butter over moderate heat in a heavy 8- to 10-inch skillet.
4. When the foam begins to subside, add the cabbage, and cook, stirring constantly, for a minute or two. Cover the skillet and set aside off the heat.
5. Drain the potatoes and return them to the pan. Shake over low heat until they are dry and mealy.
6. Then mash them to a smooth purée with a fork, a potato ricer or an electric mixer.
7. Beat into them the remaining 2 tablespoons of butter and then 1/2 cup of the milk, 2 tablespoons at a time. Use up to 1/2 cup more milk if necessary to make a purée thick enough to hold its shape in a spoon.
8. Stir in the cooked cabbage and the scallions, and add the salt and a few grindings of pepper. Taste for seasoning.
9. Then transfer the *colcannon* to a heated serving bowl, sprinkle with parsley, and serve at once.

Dutchess Potatoes

Herzoginnen Kartoffeln   *To serve 8 to 10*

3 pounds potatoes
5 tablespoons butter
1 1/2 teaspoons salt
1/4 teaspoon pepper
1/4 teaspoon nutmeg
3 egg yolks, beaten
2 whole eggs, beaten

1. Peel the potatoes, cut them in half and cook in boiling salted water to cover until they are tender.
2. Drain well, then put them through a potato ricer or mash them in an electric mixer.
3. Beat in the butter, salt, pepper, nutmeg, egg yolks and eggs until the potatoes are fluffy.
4. Put them through a pastry tube onto a heatproof serving dish or heap them in a mound.
5. Place the dish under the broiler until the potatoes are lightly browned.

Potatoes in Cheese and Chili Sauce

Papas a la Huancaina   *To serve 8*

1/4 cup fresh lemon juice
1 1/2 teaspoons crumbled, seeded, dried hot red chili, or 3 *pequín* chilies, crumbled
1 teaspoon salt
Freshly ground black pepper
1 large onion, peeled, thinly sliced, and separated into rings
8 medium boiling potatoes, peeled
1 cup coarsely crumbled *queso blanco*, or substitute 1 cup coarsely grated fresh *mozzarella* or Münster cheese
2/3 cup cup heavy cream
1 teaspoon tumeric
2 teaspoons finely chopped, seeded fresh

red or green hot chili
⅓ cup olive oil
1 fresh red or green hot chili, stemmed, seeded and cut lengthwise into ⅛-inch strips
4 hard-cooked eggs, cut lengthwise into halves
8 black olives
Bibb or Boston lettuce leaves

NOTE: Wear rubber gloves when handling the hot chilies.

1. In a large mixing bowl, combine the lemon juice, 1½ teaspoons of dried chili or the *pequín* chilies, ½ teaspoon of salt and a few grindings of black pepper.

2. Add the onion rings, turning them about with a spoon to coat them evenly with the mixture.

3. Cover the bowl and set aside to marinate at room temperaure while you boil the potatoes.

4. Drop the potatoes into a large pot of light-ly salted boiling water (enough to cover them completely), and boil the potatoes briskly until they are tender but not falling apart.

5. Meanwhile, make the sauce by combining the cheese, cream, turmeric, chopped fresh chili, ½ teaspoon salt, and a few grindings of pepper in the jar of a blender.

6. Blend at high speed for 30 seconds, or until smooth and creamy. (To make the sauce by hand, beat the ingredients together until they are well combined.) In a heavy 10-inch skillet, heat the olive oil over moderate heat.

7. Pour in the cheese and cream sauce, reduce the heat to low, and cook, stirring constantly, for 5 to 8 minutes, or until the sauce thickens.

8. To assemble, arrange the potatoes on a heated platter and pour the sauce over them.

9. Drain the onion rings and strew the rings and fresh chili strips over the potatoes.

10. Garnish with eggs, black olives and lettuce.

The potato has been a staple of the Peruvian diet since the time of the Inca. This modern dish is *papas a la huancaina,* made with cheese and chilies.

Potato Paprika

Paprikás Burgonya *To serve 4 to 6*

2 pounds boiling potatoes
3 tablespoons lard
⅔ cup finely chopped onions
¼ teaspoon finely chopped garlic
1 tablespoon sweet Hungarian paprika
**2 cups chicken or beef stock, fresh or
  canned, or 2 cups water**
⅛ teaspoon caraway seeds
**1 medium-sized tomato, peeled, seeded
  and chopped (about ¼ cup)**
**1 large green pepper with seeds and ribs
  removed, finely chopped**
1 teaspoon salt
Freshly ground black pepper
1 pound Hungarian sausage
½ cup sour cream

1. Cook the potatoes in boiling water for 8
to 10 minutes, then peel and cut into ¼-inch
slices.
2. In a 4-quart saucepan or casserole, heat
the lard until a light haze forms over it, then
add the onions and garlic. Cook for 8 to 10
minutes, or until lightly colored.
3. Off the heat, stir in paprika. Stir until the
onions are well coated.
4. Return the pan to the heat, add stock or
water, bring to a boil, and add caraway seeds,
potatoes, tomato, green pepper, salt and a
few grindings of pepper.
5. Bring the liquid to a boil, stir, cover and
simmer for 25 to 30 minutes until the potatoes
are tender.

NOTE: The addition of Debreceni or another
semisoft smoked sausage to potato paprika
makes the dish a complete meal. Slice the
sausage about ⅛ inch thick and add it when
you add the potatoes.

6. Serve in a casserole as a vegetable or en-
trée for a luncheon dish. Top each portion
with a tablespoon of sour cream.

Potato Pudding

Imellytetty Perunavuoka *To serve 8*

3 pounds potatoes
2 tablespoons sugar
4 tablespoon flour
4 teaspoons salt
3 cups milk
¼ cup melted butter

1. Wash the unpeeled potatoes and cook
them in boiling water until they are tender.
2. Drain, peel the potatoes while they are hot,
then mash them in a mixing bowl until they
are smooth.
3. Beat in the sugar and 3 tablespoons of the
flour. Sprinkle the top with the remaining
flour, cover the bowl with a cloth, and let the
potatoes stand for 3 hours, stirring
occasionally.
4. Preheat the oven to 375°.
5. Add the salt, milk and melted butter to the
potatoes, beat well, then turn the mixture into a buttered baking dish.
6. Bake for 25 minutes, or until the potatoes
are browned on top.

Potatoes with Kale

Grünkohl mit Kartoffeln *To serve 4 to 6*

9 tablespoons butter, softened
3 pound kale
½ pound lean bacon, coarsely diced
**½ cup beef or chicken stock, fresh or
  canned**
2 teaspoons salt
¼ teaspoon ground nutmeg
**9 medium-sized boiling potatoes (about 3
  pounds), peeled and cut into ½-inch
  cubes**
½ to ¾ cup milk
Freshly ground black pepper
2 egg yolks

1. With a pastry brush, coat the bottom and sides of an 8-by-10 inch baking dish with 1 tablespoon of softened butter. Set the dish aside.

2. Wash the kale thoroughly under cold running water. With a small, sharp knife, cut away the ends and the tough stems as well as any bruised or yellow leaves.

3. Drop the kale into enough lightly salted boiling water to cover it completely and boil briskly for 10 minutes.

4. Drain thoroughly in a colander, and with the back of a spoon press it firmly to remove any excess liquid; then chop the kale coarsely.

5. In a heavy 4- to 5-quart saucepan, cook the bacon over moderate heat until it is crisp and brown.

6. Add the kale, turning it about with a large spoon until the leaves are coated with the fat.

7. Then stir in the stock, 1 teaspoon of the salt and nutmeg, and bring to a boil over high heat.

8. Reduce the heat to low and simmer uncovered, stirring occasionally, for 20 minutes.

9. Meanwhile, preheat the oven to 400°.

10. Drop the potatoes into enough lightly salted boiling water to cover them completely, and boil them briskly, uncovered, until they are tender but not falling apart.

11. Drain thoroughly, return them to the pan and shake them over low heat for 2 to 3 minutes until they are dry. Then force the potatoes through a food mill or ricer set over a bowl.

12. A tablespoon at a time, beat 6 tablespoons at a time, using as much of the milk as you need to make a purée thick enough to hold its shape in a spoon.

13. Beat in the remaining teaspoon of salt, a few grindings of black pepper and the egg yolks, one at a time. Taste for seasoning.

14. Spread the cooked kale evenly over the bottom of the prepared baking dish, smooth the potatoes over it and dot the top with the remaining 2 tablespoons of butter cut into small pieces.

15. Bake in the middle of the oven for 20 minutes, or until the surface of the potatoes is golden brown.

16. Serve at once, directly from the baking dish.

Scalloped Potatoes with Cheese

Pommes de Terre Dauphinoises　　　　*To serve 6*

1 garlic clove, peeled and brushed with the flat of a knife
2½ pounds firm boiling potatoes, old or new, peeled and cut into ⅛-inch slices (about 8 cups)
1½ cups grated, imported Swiss cheese
6 tablespoons butter, cut in ¼-inch bits
1 teaspoon salt
⅛ teaspoon coarsely ground black pepper
1¼ cups milk

1. Preheat the oven to 425°.

2. Rub the bottom and sides of a flameproof baking-and-serving dish, 10 to 12 inches across and 2 inches deep, with the bruised garlic, and grease it lightly with butter.

3. Dry the potato slices with a paper towel, then spread half of the slices in the bottom of the dish. Sprinkle them with half the cheese, butter bits, salt and pepper.

4. Spread the rest of the slices in the dish and sprinkle the remaining cheese, butter, salt and pepper on top. Pour the milk into the side of the dish.

5. Bring to a simmer over low heat and then bake in the upper third of the oven for 20 minutes, or until the potatoes are almost tender when pierced with the tip of a sharp knife. At this point remove any residual liquid with a bulb baster and bake for another 5 minutes, or until the potatoes are tender, the milk absorbed, and the top nicely browned.

6. Serve at once.

Chili Potatoes with Shrimp and Vegetables

Causa a la Limeña   *To serve 8*

**3 pounds baking potatoes, peeled and
  quartered**

THE SAUCE

½ cup finely chopped onions

½ cup fresh lemon juice

**1 teaspoon finely chopped, seeded fresh
  hot chili**

1 tablespoon salt

⅛ teaspoon freshly ground black pepper

A pinch of Cayenne pepper

1 cup olive oil

THE GARNISH

**1 pound sweet potatoes, peeled, cut in half
  lengthwise and then crosswise into
  ¼-inch slices**

**1 pound fresh *yuca*, peeled, sliced
  crosswise and cut into small wedges**

8 raw jumbo shrimp in their shells

**4 ears of fresh corn, shucked and cut into
  4 rounds each**

**4 hard-cooked eggs, cut lengthwise into
  halves**

16 pitted black olives

**½ pound *queso blanco*, fresh *mozzarella* or
  Münster cheese, sliced ½ inch thick and
  cut into triangles about 2 inches long and
  1 inch wide**

NOTE: Wear rubber gloves when handling the hot chilies.

1. Preheat the oven to 250°.

2. Drop the potatoes into a large pot of lightly salted boiling water (enough to cover them) and boil them briskly until they are tender.

3. Meanwhile, make the sauce by combining the onions, lemon juice, fresh chili, salt, black pepper, Cayenne pepper, and oil, and beat them together with a whisk or fork.

4. Drain the potatoes and mash them to a smooth purée with a fork, potato masher or electric mixer.

5. Beat in the sauce, a tablespoon at a time, and taste for seasoning.

6. Mound the potatoes in the center of a large heatproof platter and cover the platter loosely with foil. Keep the potatoes warm in the preheated oven.

7. Into each of two 3- to 4-quart saucepans pour about 2 quarts of water. Bring to a boil and drop in the sweet potatoes and *yuca*.

8. Boil briskly, uncovered, for 20 minutes, or until the vegetables are tender.

9. Then remove them from their pans with a slotted spoon and arrange them around the mashed potatoes.

10. Cover the platter again and return it to the oven.

11. In a heavy 3-quart saucepan, bring 4 cups of water to a boil over high heat.

12. Drop in the shrimp and cook them, uncovered, for 5 to 8 minutes, or until they are firm and pink.

13. Drain them and peel off their shells. If desired, devein them by making a shallow incision down their backs with a small knife and lifting out the black or white intestinal vein.

14. While the shrimp cook, bring 2 quarts of water to a boil over high heat in a 4-quart saucepan.

15. Drop in the corn and boil, uncovered, for 5 to 10 minutes, until the corn is tender. Drain in a colander.

16. Remove the platter from the oven and place the corn on it.

17. Alternate the shrimp and cheese triangles in a circular design on top of the potatoes.

18. Add the olives and eggs to the arrangement, and serve at once.

Mashed potatoes are garnished with shrimp, ripe olives, cheese, corn and sweet potatoes in this wheel-shaped South American delicacy, *causa a la limeña*.

Potatoes with Onions and Anchovies

Jansson's Frestelse *To serve 4 to 6*

7 medium boiling potatoes, peeled and cut into strips 2 inches long and ¼ inch thick
2½ tablespoons butter
2 tablespoons vegetable oil
2 to 3 large yellow onions, thinly sliced (4 cups)
16 flat anchovy fillets, drained
White pepper
2 tablespoons fine dry bread crumbs
2 tablespoons butter, cut into ¼-inch bits
1 cup heavy cream
½ cup milk

1. Preheat the oven to 400°.
2. Place the potato strips in cold water to keep them from discoloring.
3. Heat 2 tablespoons of butter and 2 tablespoons of oil in a 10- to 12-inch skillet; when the foam subsides, add the onions and cook 10 minutes, stirring frequently, until they are soft but not brown.
4. With a pastry brush or paper towel, spread a 1½- to 2-quart soufflé dish or baking dish with the remaining half tablespoon of butter.
5. Drain the potatoes and pat them dry with paper towels.
6. Arrange a layer of potatoes on the bottom of the dish and then alternate layers of onions and anchovies, ending with potatoes. Sprinkle each layer with a little white pepper.
7. Scatter bread crumbs over the top layer of potatoes and dot the casserole with the 2 tablespoons of butter cut into bits.
8. In a small saucepan, heat the milk and cream until it barely simmers, then pour over the potatoes.
9. Bake in the center of the oven for 45 minutes, or until the potatoes are tender when pierced with the tip of a sharp knife and the liquid is nearly absorbed.

Roasted Potatoes

Hasselbackpotatis *To serve 6*

6 baking potatoes, about 4 inches long and 2 inches wide
1 tablespoon soft butter
3 tablespoons melted butter
1 teaspoon salt
2 tablespoons dry bread crumbs
2 tablespoons grated imported Parmesan cheese (optional)

1. Preheat the oven to 425°
2. Peel the potatoes and drop them into a bowl of cold water to prevent them from discoloring.
3. Place one potato at a time on a wooden spoon large enough to cradle it comfortably, and beginning at about ½ inch from the end, slice down at ⅛-inch intervals. (The deep, curved bowl of the wooden spoon will prevent the knife from slicing completely through the potato.)
4. Drop each semisliced potato back into the cold water.
5. When you are ready to roast them, drain the potatoes and pat them dry with paper towels.
6. With a pastry brush or paper towels, generously butter a baking dish large enough to hold the potatoes side by side in one layer and arrange them in it cut side up.
7. Baste the potatoes with 1½ tablespoons of the melted butter, sprinkle them liberally with salt, and set them in the center of the oven.
8. After 30 minutes sprinkle a few of the bread crumbs over the surface of each potato, baste with the remaining melted butter and the butter in the pan, and continue to roast another 15 minutes, or until the potatoes are golden brown and show no resistance when pierced with the tip of a sharp knife.
9. If you wish to use the cheese, it should be strewn over the potatoes 5 minutes before they are done.

Roasted Potato Wedges

Brynt Potatis i Ugn   To serve 4 to 6

4 medium-sized baking potatoes
4 tablespoons melted butter
Salt

1. Preheat the oven to 450°.
2. Peel the potatoes and cut them in half lengthwise. Stand each half upright on a chopping board and slice it in thirds down its length, making 3 wedge-shaped pieces.
3. Blanch the wedges by cooking them rapidly for 3 minutes in enough unsalted boiling water to cover them. Drain and pat them dry with paper towels.
4. With a pastry brush or paper towels, butter a baking dish large enough to hold the potatoes side by side in a single layer.
5. Dribble melted butter over the tops and sprinkle them liberally with salt.
6. Roast them in the center of the oven for 15 minutes, turn them, and roast another 15 minutes.
7. These crisp potato wedges make excellent accompaniments to roasted meats or poultry.

Game Chips

     To serve 4 to 6

4 cups vegetable oil or shortening
6 medium-sized baking potatoes (about 2
   pounds), peeled
2 teaspoons salt

1. Preheat the oven to 250°.
2. Line a jelly-roll pan or large, shallow roasting pan with a double thickness of paper towels, and set it aside.
3. In a deep-fat fryer or large, heavy saucepan, heat the oil to 360° on a deep-frying thermometer, or until a haze forms above it.
4. With a large knife or a vegetable slicer, cut the potatoes into slices $\frac{1}{16}$ inch thick and drop them directly into cold water to remove the starch and prevent them from discoloring.
5. When ready to use, drain them in a colander, spread them out in a single layer on paper towels, and pat them thoroughly dry with more towels.
6. Drop about $\frac{1}{2}$ cup of the potatoes at a time into the hot fat and, turning the slices about with a slotted spoon, fry for 2 or 3 minutes, or until they are crisp and golden brown.
7. Transfer the chips to the paper-lined pan and keep them warm in the oven while you proceed with the remaining batches.
8. To serve, heap the chips in a heated bowl and sprinkle them with the salt. Game chips are traditionally served with roasted birds, such as pheasant, in which case they may be arranged in a circle around the bird.

Portuguese Fried Potatoes

Batatas à Portuguêsa   To serve 4

3 tablespoons butter
3 tablespoons olive oil
1½ pounds new potatoes, peeled and
   sliced into ¼-inch-thick rounds
½ teaspoon salt
Freshly ground black pepper
1 tablespoon finely chopped parsley

1. In a heavy 10- to 12-inch skillet, melt the butter in the olive oil over moderate heat. When the foam begins to subside, add the potatoes.
2. Turning them frequently with a metal spatula, cook for 15 minutes or until they are tender and golden brown.
3. Season with salt and a few grindings of pepper, then transfer the potatoes to a heated bowl or platter and serve at once, sprinkled with parsley if you like.

Grated potatoes spiced with chives, salt and pepper, and heated in a hot skillet, are transformed into the Swedish pancakes called *rårakor*.

Potato Pancakes with Chives

Rårakor med Gräslök   *To serve 4*

4 medium-sized baking potatoes
2 tablespoons chopped fresh chives
2 teaspoons salt
Freshly ground black pepper
2 to 4 tablespoons butter
2 to 4 tablespoons vegetable oil

1. Peel the potatoes and grate them coarsely, preferably into tiny slivers, into a large mixing bowl. Do not drain off the potato water that will accumulate in the bowl.

2. Work quickly to prevent the potatoes from turning brown, mix into them the chopped chives, salt and a few grindings of pepper.

3. Heat the butter and oil in a 10- to 12-inch skillet over high heat until the foam subsides. The pan must be very hot, but not smoking.

4. Using 2 tablespoons of potato mixture for each pancake, fry 3 or 4 at a time, flattening them out with a spatula to about 3 inches in diameter.

5. Fry each batch over medium-high heat for 2 or 3 minutes on each side, or until they are crisp and golden. Add more butter and oil, if necessary, after each batch.

Sautéed Potato Balls

Pommes de Terre Noisette   *To serve 6 to 8*

3 pounds potatoes
3 tablespoons oil
6 tablespoons butter
1 teaspoon salt
1 tablespoon minced parsley

1. Peel and wash the potatoes.
2. With the small end of a melon ball cutter, scoop them into little balls.
3. Heat the oil and half the butter in a skillet.
4. When the foam subsides add the potato balls and cook them over medium heat until they are light gold in color, shaking the pan frequently.
5. Add the salt, then cover and cook over low heat for 10 minutes, or until the potatoes are tender, shaking the pan a few times.
6. Add the parsley and the remaining butter, shaking the pan until the butter melts.
7. Serve at once.

Hashed Brown Potatoes

To serve 4 to 6

6 medium-sized boiling potatoes (about 2
** pounds), peeled and cut into quarters**
¼ pound sliced bacon
2 tablespoons butter
1 teaspoon salt
Freshly ground black pepper

1. Bring 2 quarts of lightly salted water to a boil in a 4- to 5-quart pot and boil the potatoes uncovered until they can be easily pierced with the tip of a small, sharp knife.
2. Drain the potatoes in a colander, return to the pan in which they were cooked or put

them in a large, dry skillet and shake over moderate heat until they are dry.
3. Let the potatoes cool, then cut them into small dice.
4. In a heavy 10- to 12-inch skillet, preferably one with a good nonstick surface, cook the bacon until it has rendered all of its fat and is crisp and brown.
5. Remove the bacon with a slotted spoon and drain on paper towels.
6. Add the butter to the bacon fat and place over moderate heat until the butter melts.
7. Add the potatoes, and sprinkle them with the salt and a few grindings of black pepper. Then press the potatoes down firmly into the pan with a spatula.
8. Cook over moderate heat, shaking the pan occasionally to prevent the potatoes from sticking. A brown crust should form on the bottom surface of the potatoes in about 20 minutes. Check by gently lifting the edge of the potatoes with a spatula.
9. Cook a few minutes longer, raising the heat if necessary to achieve the proper color. They should be golden brown and crusty.
10. To serve, cover the skillet with a heated platter and, grasping skillet and plate together, turn them upside down. The potatoes should fall out easily.
11. Serve at once, sprinkled with the crumbled reserved bacon if desired.

Rutabaga Casserole

Länttulaatikko To serve 8

2½ pounds (about 2) rutabagas, peeled and cut into ¼-inch dice (8 cups) or substitute 2½ pounds white or yellow turnips, peeled and diced into ¼-inch pieces
3 teaspoons salt
¼ cup dry bread crumbs
¼ cup heavy cream
½ teaspoon nutmeg
2 eggs, lightly beaten
2 tablespoons plus 2 teaspoons soft butter
2 tablespoons butter, cut into tiny bits

1. Preheat the oven to 350°.
2. Place the 8 cups of diced rutabagas (or diced turnips) in a 4- to 6-quart stainless-steel or enameled saucepan. Pour in enough cold water to just cover the vegetables, add 1 teaspoon of salt and bring to a boil.
3. Lower the heat and simmer, partially covered, for 15 to 20 minutes, or until the rutabagas offer no resistance when pierced with the tip of a sharp knife.
4. Drain the rutabagas and, with the back of a spoon, force them through a sieve set over a bowl.
5. In another bowl, soak the bread crumbs in the heavy cream for a few minutes.
6. Stir in the nutmeg, 2 teaspoons of the salt and the lightly beaten eggs, then add the puréed rutabagas and mix together thoroughly.
7. Stir in 2 tablespoons of the soft butter.
8. Spread a 2- to 2½-quart casserole or baking dish with 2 teaspoons of soft butter and transfer the rutabaga mixture to the casserole.
9. Dot with the bits of butter and bake uncovered for 1 hour, or until the top is lightly browned.
10. Serve hot, as an accompaniment to pork or ham.

Sauerkraut with Wine and Grapes

Weinkraut To serve 6

2 pounds fresh sauerkraut
2 tablespoons bacon fat
2 cups dry white wine
½ pound seedless green grapes

1. Drain the sauerkraut, wash it thoroughly under cold running water, and then let it soak in a pot of water for 10 to 20 minutes, depending upon its acidity. A handful at a time, squeeze the sauerkraut until it is completely dry.
2. In a heavy 3-quart casserole or saucepan, heat the bacon fat over moderate heat until a light haze forms above it. Add the sauerkraut and cook for serveral minutes, separating the strands with a fork.
3. Pour in the wine, and bring it to a boil.
4. Then reduce the heat to its lowest point, cover the casserole, and simmer for 1½ to 2 hours, or until the sauerkraut has absorbed most of the wine. (If at any point during the cooking the sauerkraut seems dry, add a few tablespoons of wine from time to time.)
5. Stir in the grapes, cover the casserole again, and simmer for 10 minutes longer.
6. Serve a once from a heated platter or serving bowl.

Sauerkraut mixed with pineapple and served in the shell of the fruit is both decorative and a surprisingly appetizing addition to a meal.

Pineapple Sauerkraut

Sauerkraut mit Ananas   *To serve 6 to 8*

2 pounds fresh sauerkraut
5 cups unsweetened pineapple juice
  (2 twenty-ounce cans)
A 1½- to 2-pound ripe pineapple

1. Drain the sauerkraut, wash it thoroughly under cold running water, and let it soak in a pot of cold water for 10 to 20 minutes, depending upon its acidity. A handful at a time, squeeze the sauerkraut until it is completely dry.
2. Combine the sauerkraut and pineapple juice in a heavy 3- to 4-quart saucepan, and bring to a boil over high heat, stirring with a fork to separate the sauerkraut strands.
3. Reduce the heat to it lowest point and cover the pan tightly. Simmer, undisturbed, for 1½ to 2 hours, or until the sauerkraut has absorbed most of its cooking liquid.
4. With a long, sharp knife, cut the top 1½ inches off the pineapple and set the top aside.
5. Hollow out the pineapple carefully, leaving a ⅛- to ¼-inch layer of the fruit in the shell.
6. Remove and discard the woody core of the hollowed-out fruit and cut the fruit into ½-inch cubes.
7. Stir the diced pineapple into the cooked sauerkraut, cook for a minute or two, then pour the entire mixture into a large sieve set over bowl.
8. When all the liquid has drained through, pile the sauerkraut into the pineapple shell.
9. Cover with the reserved pineapple top and serve on a large plate.
10. If you like, any remaining sauerkraut may be presented mounded on the plate around the pineapple.

Spinach Mold

Sformato di Spinaci   *To serve 4 to 6*

5 tablespoons butter
2 tablespoons fine dry bread crumbs, made from French or Italian bread
3 tablespoons finely chopped onions
1 ten-ounce package chopped frozen spinach, thoroughly defrosted, squeezed dry and chopped again — or ¾ pound fresh spinach, cooked, drained, squeezed and finely chopped
3 tablespoons flour
1 cup milk
Freshly ground black pepper
3 egg yolks
¼ cup freshly grated imported Parmesan cheese
Salt
3 egg whites

1. With 1 tablespoon of butter, grease the top pan of a double boiler (it should be large enough to hold at least 1 quart), or preheat the oven to 325° and butter a 1-quart charlotte mold or other plain metal mold with a cover.

2. Dust the bottom and sides of the pan with bread crumbs and tap the pan lightly to knock out the excess.

3. In a heavy 8- to 10-inch skillet, melt 2 tablespoons of butter over moderate heat and in it cook the onions, stirring frequently, for 7 or 8 minutes, or until they are transparent but not browned.

4. Stir in the spinach and cook, stirring constantly, for 2 or 3 minutes. When all of the moisture has cooked away and the spinach begins to stick lightly to the pan, remove the skillet from the heat.

5. Melt the remaining 2 tablespoons of the butter in a heavy 3- to 4-quart saucepan.

6. Remove from the heat and stir in the flour. Then pour in the milk, stirring with a whisk until the flour is partially dissolved.

7. Return the pan to low heat and cook, stirring constantly, until the sauce boils and becomes thick and smooth.

8. Remove from the heat and beat in the egg yolks, one at a time, whisking until each one is thoroughly blended before adding the next.

9. Stir in the cheese and the onion-and-spinach mixture, and season with salt and pepper to taste. Allow it to cool slightly.

10. Now beat the egg whites until they are stiff enough to form unwavering peaks when the beater is lifted from the bowl.

11. Stir a heaping spoonful of egg whites into the sauce to lighten it, then gently fold in the remaining egg whites. Ladle the mixture into the buttered pan or mold.

12. To cook the *sformato* in the double boiler, place the top pan in simmering water deep enough to come almost all the way up its sides Cover and cook slowly over barely simmering water.

13. To cook in the oven, place the mold in a pot and add enough simmering water to reach about ¾ of the way up the sides of the mold. Cover and bake on the middle shelf of the oven, regulating the heat to keep the water at the barest simmer.

14. Either way, the *sformato* should be just firm to the touch in about 1 hour.

15. To serve, uncover the pan and wipe the outside dry.

16. Run a knife or narrow spatula around the inside of the pan.

17. Place a serving plate upside down over the top of the pan and, grasping both sides firmly, invert the two.

18. Rap the plate sharply on the table and the *sformato* will slide out easily.

19. Serve at once.

Spinach, eggs and *feta* cheese are combined with many layers of thin *filo* pastry to make a flaky, melt-in-the-mouth Greek pie. The recipe is below.

Spinach and Cheese Pie

Spanakopita   *To serve 6 to 8*

¼ cup olive oil
½ cup finely chopped onions
¼ cup finely chopped scallions, including
    2 inches of the green tops
2 pounds fresh spinach, washed,
    thoroughly drained and finely chopped
¼ cup finely cut fresh dill leaves, or
    substitute 2 tablespoons dried dill weed
¼ cup finely chopped parsley, preferably
    flat-leaf parsley
½ teaspoon salt
Freshly ground black pepper
⅓ cup milk
½ pound *feta* cheese, finely crumbled
4 eggs, lightly beaten
½ pound butter, melted
16 sheets (½ pound) *filo* pastry, each
    about 16 inches long and 12 inches wide

1. In a heavy 10- to 12-inch skillet, heat the olive oil over moderate heat until a light haze forms above it.
2. Add the onions and scallions and, stirring frequently, cook for 5 minutes, or until they are soft and transparent but not brown.
3. Stir in the spinach, cover tightly, and cook for 5 minutes.
4. Then add the dill, parsley, salt and a few grindings of pepper and, stirring and shaking the pan almost constantly, cook uncovered for about 10 minutes, or until most of the liquid in the skillet has evaporated and the spinach has begun to stick lightly to the pan.
5. Transfer the spinach mixture to a deep bowl and stir in the milk. Cool to room temperature, then add the cheese and slowly beat in the eggs. Taste for seasoning.
6. Preheat the oven to 300°.
7. With a pastry brush, coat the bottom and sides of a 12-by-7-by-2-inch baking dish with melted butter.
8. Line the dish with a sheet of *filo*, pressing the edges of the pastry firmly into the corners and against the sides of the dish.
9. Brush the entire surface of the pastry with about 2 or 3 teaspoons of the remaining butter, spreading it all the way to the outside edges and lay another sheet of *filo* on top.
10. Spread with another 2 or 3 teaspoons of butter and continue constructing the pie in this fashion until you have used 8 layers of the *filo* in all.
11. With a rubber spatula, spread the spinach mixture evenly over the last layer of *filo* and smooth it into the corners.
12. Then place another sheet of the *filo* on top, coat with butter, and repeat with the remaining layers of *filo* and butter as before.
13. Trim the excess pastry from around the rim of the dish with scissors.
14. Brush the top of the pie with the remaining butter and bake in the middle of the oven for 1 hour, or until the pastry is crisp and delicately browned.
15. Cut into squares and serve hot or at room temperature.

Spinach in Cheese Sauce

To serve 6

3 pounds fresh spinach
1 cup milk
2 tablespoons flour
2 tablespoons melted butter
Salt
Pepper
1 cup grated cheese

1. Preheat the oven to 350°.
2. Soak the spinach in salted water for a few minutes to freshen it. Cut off the roots and wilted leaves. Wash thoroughly until no sand can be found in the bottom of the pan.
3. Cook the spinach in a covered pan with only the water that drips from the leaves. When its crispness is gone, drain the spinach and place it in a baking dish.
4. Meanwhile, heat the milk in the top of a double boiler.
5. Blend together the flour and melted butter, then stir the mixture into the hot milk. Season to taste with salt and pepper.
6. When the mixture begins to thicken, add the grated cheese. Stir until the cheese has melted and the sauce is smooth.
7. Pour the sauce over the spinach and bake until it is browned.

Spinach with Pine Nuts and Almonds

Espinacas con Piñones y Almendras   *To serve 4*

¼ cup olive oil
1 large garlic clove, peeled and cut in half lengthwise
¼ cup pine nuts *(pignoli)*
¼ cup blanched slivered almonds
1 pound freshly cooked spinach, drained and finely chopped, or 2 ten-ounce packages chopped frozen spinach, thoroughly defrosted and drained

¼ cup finely diced *serrano* ham or substitute
1 ounce prosciutto or other lean smoked ham
1 teaspoon salt

1. In a heavy 10- to 12-inch skillet, heat the olive oil over moderate heat until a light haze forms above it.
2. Add the garlic and, stirring constantly, cook for 1 or 2 minutes.
3. Remove the garlic with a slotted spoon and discard it.
4. Add the pine nuts and almonds to the oil remaining in the pan and cook for 2 or 3 minutes, or until they are slightly brown.
5. Add the spinach, ham and salt and toss together with a spoon until the ingredients are thoroughly mixed and heated through.
6. Taste for seasoning and serve at once.

Spiced Acorn Squash

To serve 8

4 medium-sized acorn squash
½ cup dark brown sugar
1 teaspoon cinnamon
½ teaspoon grated nutmeg
¼ teaspoon ground cloves
½ teaspoon salt
8 tablespoons melted butter (1 quarter-pound stick)
½ cup maple syrup
Eight ½-inch pieces of bacon
About 2 cups boiling water

1. Preheat the oven to 350°.
2. Cut each squash in half and with a teaspoon scrape out the seeds and fibers.
3. In a small bowl combine the brown sugar, cinnamon, nutmeg, cloves, salt and melted butter, and stir them together thoroughly.
4. Arrange the squash in a shallow ovenproof baking dish large enough to hold them all comfortably.

(continued on page 60)

5. Spoon an equal amount of the spiced butter mixture into the hollow of each squash and over that pour a teaspoon or so of maple syrup. Top with a piece of bacon.

6. Now add boiling water to the baking dish – the water should be about 1 inch deep.

7. Bake in the middle of the oven for about 1 hour, or until the squash can be easily pierced with the tip of a small, sharp knife.

8. Serve at once.

Acorn Squash with Yams

To serve 12

6 acorn squash
4 tablespoons butter
Salt
Pepper
2 cans yams
1 egg
4 tablespoons finely chopped ginger
½ cup grated Parmesan cheese

1. Preheat the oven to 350°.

2. Cut the squash in half crosswise and remove the seeds.

3. Melt 2 tablespoons of the butter and brush it on the squash. Season to taste with salt and pepper.

4. Place the squash on a cookie sheet and bake for 50 to 60 minutes, or until the flesh is soft.

5. Remove the squash from the oven and carefully scoop out the flesh, reserving the shells.

6. Drain the yams and force them and the squash through a strainer into a bowl. Beat in the egg and the ginger.

7. Fill the squash shells with this mixture, sprinkle with the cheese and dot with the remaining butter.

8. Brown under the broiler and serve.

Glazed Sweet Potatoes

To serve 6

6 sweet potatoes
½ cup brown sugar
½ teaspoon salt
4 tablespoons butter
¼ cup water

1. Preheat the oven to 400°.

2. Boil the sweet potatoes is salted water until they are tender.

3. Peel the potatoes, cut them in half lengthwise, and place them in an oiled baking pan.

4. Sprinkle them with the sugar and salt, and dot with the butter.

5. Add the water to the pan.

6. Bake, turning frequently, for about 20 minutes, or until the potatoes are brown.

Tomatoes Stuffed with Rice

Domates Yemistes me Rizi   *To serve 6*

1¼ cups water
½ cup uncooked long- or medium-grained rice
6 firm ripe tomatoes, each about 3 inches in diameter
2 teaspoons salt
6 tablespoons olive oil
½ cup finely chopped onions
¾ cup canned tomato purée
½ cup finely chopped parsley, preferably flat-leaf parsley
2 tablespoons finely cut fresh mint, or substitute 1 tablespoon dried mint
2 teaspoons finely chopped garlic
¼ teaspoon oregano, crumbled
Freshly ground black pepper

(continued on page 62)

1. In a small saucepan, bring 1 cup of water to a boil over high heat.

2. Pour in the rice in a slow thin stream, stir once or twice, and cook briskly uncovered for 8 minutes, or until the rice is softened but still somewhat resistant to the bite.

3. Drain the rice in a sieve and set aside.

4. Cut a ¼-inch slice off the tops of the tomatoes and set aside.

5. With a spoon, hollow out the tomatoes, remove the inner pulp and discard the seeds. Chop the pulp and set it aside.

6. Sprinkle the tomato cavities with 1 teaspoon of salt and turn them upside down on paper towels to drain.

7. Preheat the oven to 350°.

8. Make the stuffing in the following fashion: In a heavy 10- to 12-inch skillet, heat the oil over moderate heat until a light haze forms above it.

9. Add the onions and, stirring frequently, cook for 5 minutes, or until they are soft and transparent but not brown.

10. Stir in the rice, tomato pulp, ½ cup of the tomato purée, the parsley, mint, garlic, oregano, the remaining teaspoon of salt and a few grindings of pepper.

11. Stirring constantly, cook briskly until most of the liquid in the pan evaporates and the mixture is thick enough to hold its shape almost solidly in the spoon.

12. Arrange the tomatoes, cut side up, in a baking dish large enough to hold them side by side.

13. Fill the tomatoes with the stuffing, packing it in firmly, and cover each tomato with its reserved top.

14. Combine the remaining ¼ cup of tomato purée with the remaining ¼ cup of water and pour the mixture around the tomatoes.

15. Bake uncovered in the middle of the oven for 20 minutes, basting the tomatoes once or twice with the cooking liquid.

16. Cool to room temperature and serve the tomatoes directly from the baking dish.

Pennsylvania Dutch Tomatoes

To serve 4 to 6

**4 to 5 large firm ripe tomatoes, 3 to 4
    inches in diameter, thickly sliced**
2 teaspoons salt
Freshly ground black pepper
½ cup flour
4 to 6 tablespoons butter
2 tablespoons sifted brown sugar
1 cup heavy cream
1 tablespoon finely chopped fresh parsley

1. Sprinkle the tomatoes on both sides with salt and a few grindings of black pepper. Then dip tomato slices in the flour, coating each side thoroughly and very gently shaking off any excess.

2. In a 12-inch heavy skillet, preferably of the nonstick variety, melt the butter over moderate heat.

3. When the foam subsides, add the tomato slices and cook them for about 5 minutes, or until they are lightly browned.

4. Sprinkle the tops with half the brown sugar, carefully turn the tomatoes over with a spatula and sprinkle with the rest of the brown sugar.

5. Cook for 3 to 4 minutes, then transfer the slices to a heated serving platter.

6. Pour the cream into the pan, raise the heat to high and bring the cream to a boil, stirring constantly.

7. Boil briskly for 2 to 3 minutes, or until the cream thickens.

8. Taste for seasoning, then pour over the tomatoes. Sprinkle with the finely chopped parsley.

NOTE: Traditionally, this recipe is made with green tomatoes; however, they are not easily available. If you can find them, cook them somewhat more slowly and for a few minutes longer on each side.

Sherried Yams
with Pecans

To serve 6

6 medium-sized yams or sweet potatoes
½ cup brown sugar
1 cup orange juice
1 tablespoon grated orange rind
⅓ cup sherry
1 cup pecans, coarsely chopped
2 tablespoons butter

1. Boil the yams or sweet potatoes in salted water until they are tender. Peel them and cut them in thick slices.
2. Preheat the oven to 350°.
3. In a bowl, combine the sugar, orange juice, orange rind and sherry.
4. Place a layer of yams in a baking dish, cover it with some of the sherry mixture, and sprinkle generously with pecans.
5. Repeat layers of yams, liquid and pecans until the casserole is filled.
6. Pour the remaining juice over the top, sprinkle with nuts, and dot with the butter.
7. Cover and bake for 30 minutes, or until the juice has been absorbed by the yams and the top is browned.

Braised Zucchini

Courgettes Braisées   *To serve 6 to 8*

3 pounds zucchini
2 tablespoons salt
⅓ cup flour
3 tablespoons olive oil
3 tablespoons butter
½ cup broth
¼ teaspoon pepper

1. Scrub the zucchini well with a vegetable brush, then wash and dry it. Cut it in very thin slices, then place them in a bowl.
2. Sprinkle the salt over the zucchini and let it stand for 30 minutes, stirring the slices a few times.
3. Drain well, then dry the slices thoroughly with paper towels. Toss them in the flour.
4. Heat the oil and butter in a large skillet.
5. Add the floured zucchini slices and cook until they are lightly browned.
6. Add the broth and the pepper.
7. Cover the skillet and simmer for 15 minutes, or until the zucchini is tender but still crisp.

Beef-stuffed Zucchini with Tomato Sauce

Zucchini Ripieni   To serve 4 to 6

1½ cups tomato sauce (below)
4 medium-sized zucchini, scrubbed but not peeled
¼ cup olive oil
½ cup finely chopped onions
½ teaspoon finely chopped garlic
½ pound ground beef chuck
1 egg, lightly beaten
2 ounces, finely chopped prosciutto (about ¼ cup)
½ cup fresh white bread crumbs (from French or Italian bread)
6 tablespoons freshly grated imported Parmesan cheese
½ teaspoon dried oregano, crumbled
1 teaspoon salt
¼ teaspoon freshly ground black pepper

1. Prepare the tomato sauce *(below)*.
2. Preheat the oven to 375°.
3. Cut the zucchini in half lengthwise and spoon out most of the pulp, leaving hollow boatlike shells about ¼ inch thick.
4. Set the shells aside and chop the pulp coarsely.
5. Heat 3 tablespoons of olive oil in a heavy 8- to 10-inch skillet, add the onions and cook them over moderate heat for 8 to 10 minutes, or until they are soft and lightly colored.
6. Add the zucchini pulp and the garlic and cook for about 5 minutes longer, stirring frequently.
7. With a rubber spatula scrape the entire contents of the skillet into a large sieve set over a mixing bowl and let them drain.
8. Meanwhile, heat a tablespoon of oil in the skillet, add the ground beef and brown it over moderate heat, stirring almost constantly with a large fork to break up any lumps. Scrape the beef into another sieve and let it drain.
9. Now in a large mixing bowl combine the drained vegetables and meat.
10. Beat into them the lightly beaten egg, prosciutto, bread crumbs, 2 tablespoons of grated

cheese, oregano, salt and pepper and taste for seasoning.
11. Spoon this stuffing into the hollowed zucchini shells, mounding the tops slightly.
12. To bake the zucchini, use a 12-by-16-inch shallow baking dish into which 1½ cups of tomato sauce have been poured.
13. Then carefully arrange the stuffed zucchini on the sauce.
14. Sprinkle their tops with ¼ cup of cheese, dribble a few drops of olive oil over them and cover the dish tightly with aluminum foil.
15. Bring the sauce to a simmer on top of the stove, then transfer the dish to the middle of the oven and bake the zucchini for 30 minutes, removing the foil after 20 minutes so that the tops of the zucchini can brown lightly.
16. Serve directly from the baking dish.

TOMATO SAUCE
2 tablespoons olive oil
½ cup finely chopped onions
2 cups Italian plum or whole-pack tomatoes, coarsely chopped but not drained
3 tablespoons tomato paste
1 tablespoon finely cut fresh basil or 1 teaspoon dried basil
1 teaspoon sugar
½ teaspoon salt
Freshly ground black pepper

1. Using a 2- to 3-quart enameled or stainless-steel saucepan, heat the olive oil until a light haze forms over it.
2. Add the onions and cook them over moderate heat for 7 to 8 minutes, or until they are soft but not browned.
3. Add the tomatoes, tomato paste, basil, sugar, salt and a few grindings of pepper.
4. Reduce the heat to very low and simmer, with the pan partially covered, for about 40 minutes. Stir occasionally.
5. Press the sauce through a fine sieve (or a food mill) into a bowl or pan. Taste for seasoning.

Stewed Zucchini with Peppers and Tomatoes

Pisto Manchego   *To serve 4*

⅓ cup olive oil
3 cups coarsely chopped onions
2 medium-sized zucchini, scrubbed and cut into ¼-inch cubes
2 large green peppers, deribbed, seeded and coarsely chopped
2 teaspoons salt
4 medium-sized tomatoes, peeled, seeded and coarsely chopped
1 egg, lightly beaten

1. In a heavy 12-inch skillet, heat the olive oil over high heat until a light haze forms above it.

2. Add the onions, squash, peppers and salt, stir together, then cover the pan, and reduce the heat to its lowest possible point.

3. Cook for about 40 minues, or until the vegetables are tender, stirring occasionally.

4. Meanwhile, place the tomatoes in a 1- to 1½-quart saucepan and bring to a boil over moderate heat.

5. Stirring and mashing them against the sides of the pan, cook briskly, uncovered, until most of the liquid in the pan evaporates and the tomatoes become a thick, fairly smooth purée.

6. Stir them into the vegetables, then pour in the beaten egg, stirring constantly.

7. Simmer about 10 seconds but do not let the mixture boil.

8. Taste for seasoning and serve at once.

A classic Spanish vegetable dish is *pisto manchego* – zucchini, onions, tomatoes and peppers cooked almost to a purée and garnished with hard-cooked egg.

Lamb-stuffed Zucchini with Tomato Sauce

Kousa Mahshi   *To serve 6*

SAUCE

7 medium-sized fresh ripe tomatoes, peeled, seeded and finely chopped, or substitute 2½ cups chopped, drained, tomatoes
1 cup finely chopped onions
2½ cups water
1 teaspoon salt
Freshly ground black pepper

1. To make the sauce, combine the tomatoes, onions, 2½ cups of water, 1 teaspoon salt and a few grindings of pepper in a heavy casserole large enough to hold the squash in 1 or 2 layers.
2. Stirring frequently, bring to a boil over high heat, reduce the heat to low, cover and simmer for 20 minutes. Set aside.

SQUASH

6 medium-sized zucchini or other summer squash, each about 7 to 8 inches long
2 teaspoons salt
2 teaspoons finely cut fresh mint or 1 teaspoon dried mint

1. Meanwhile, scrub the zucchini under cold running water. Pat them dry with paper towels and, with a small, sharp knife, cut about 1 inch off the stem ends.
2. Carefully tunnel out the center of each squash leaving an ⅛-inch-thick shell all around. The best utensil for this is the Syrian *munara*, or squash corer, but you can use an apple corer almost as effectively.
3. As the squash are cored, drop them into a large bowl containing 2 quarts of water, 2 teaspoons of salt and the mint. Let the squash soak for 5 or 10 minutes.

STUFFING

1 pound lean ground lamb
⅔ cup uncooked long- or medium-grain white rice, thoroughly washed and drained
1 teaspoon salt
¼ teaspoon ground nutmeg, preferably freshly grated
½ teaspoon ground allspice
Freshly ground black pepper

1. To make the stuffing, combine the lamb, rice, 1 teaspoon salt, nutmeg, allspice and a few grindings of pepper.
2. Knead vigorously with both hands, then beat with a wooden spoon until the mixture is smooth and fluffy.
3. Spoon the stuffing into the squash, tapping the bottom end lightly on the table to shake the stuffing down, then filling the squash to their tops.
4. Place the squash into the tomato sauce, laying them flat.
5. Bring to a boil over high heat, reduce the heat to low, cover tightly and simmer for 30 minutes, or until the squash show only the slightest resistance when pierced with the point of a small, sharp knife. Do not overcook.
6. To serve, carefully transfer the squash to a heated platter or individual serving dishes and spoon the sauce over them.

Zucchini in Cheese Sauce

To serve 4

3 small zucchini
Salt
¼ cup milk
1 egg
⅔ cup grated cheese
4 tablespoons butter

1. Wash the zucchini and cut them crosswise into ½-inch slices.
2. Cook them in a small amount of salted water until they are soft.
3. Preheat the oven to 400°.
4. In a small bowl, beat the egg. Add the milk and grated cheese and mix well.
5. Place the zucchini in a casserole and pour the cheese sauce over it. Dot the top with the butter.
6. Bake, uncovered, until the cheese is melted and the top is nicely browned.

Marinated Vegetables, Greek Style

Légumes à la Grecque   *To serve 8 to 10*

MARINADE
3 cups chicken stock, fresh or canned
1 cup dry white wine
1 cup olive oil
½ cup lemon juice
6 parsley sprigs
2 large garlic cloves, cut up
½ teaspoon dried thyme
10 peppercorns
1 teaspoon salt

1. Stir the ingredients together in a 3- to 4-quart enameled or stainless-steel saucepan, bring to a boil, partially cover the pan and simmer slowly for 45 minutes.
2. Using a fine sieve, strain the marinade into a large bowl, pressing down hard on the ingredients with the back of a spoon to squeeze out their juices before discarding them.
3. Return the marinade to the saucepan and taste it. To be effective, the marinade should be somewhat overseasoned. This makes about 5 cups.

VEGETABLES
24 white onions, 1 inch in diameter, peeled
1 pound small zucchini, unpeeled, sliced 1 inch thick
1 pound small yellow squash, unpeeled, sliced 1 inch thick
3 medium green peppers, seeded and cut lengthwise into ½-inch strips
½ pound whole green string beans, trimmed
2 lemons, cut into ¼-inch slices

1. Bring the marinade to a boil and add the onions; cover and cook over moderate heat for 20 to 30 minutes or until the onions are just tender when pierced with the tip of a sharp knife.
2. With a slotted spoon, remove the onions to a large glass or stainless-steel baking dish.
3. Add the slices of zucchini and yellow squash to the simmering marinade and cook slowly uncovered for 10 to 15 minutes or until they are barely done, then put them in the baking dish with the onions.
4. Finally, add the green-pepper strips and string beans to the marinade and cook them slowly uncovered for 8 to 10 minutes, or until they are just tender. The vegetables must not be overcooked because they will soften as they cool and marinate.
5. Lift the green peppers and string beans out

(continued on next page)

of the pan and add them to the other vegetables.

6. Taste and season the marinade and pour it over the vegetables, making sure that they are all at least partly covered with the hot liquid.

7. Place the baking dish in the refrigerator to cool the vegetables. Then cover the dish tightly with aluminum foil or plastic wrap and let the vegetables marinate in the refrigerator for at least 4 hours – or overnight if possible – before serving them.

8. To serve, lift the vegetables out of the marinade with a slotted spoon and arrange them attractively on a serving platter. Moisten the vegetables with a little marinade and garnish them with lemon slices.

NOTE: Any other firm vegetable may be added to or substituted for those in the recipe, such as mushrooms, celery hearts, leeks, cucumbers, red peppers and artichoke hearts.

Vegetables with Yoghurt

Kheera ka Rayta   *To serve 4*

1 medium-sized cucumber
1 tablespoon finely chopped onions
1 tablespoon salt
1 small, firm ripe tomato, cut crosswise into ½-inch-thick rounds, sliced into ½-inch-wide strips and then into ½-inch cubes
1 tablespoon finely chopped fresh coriander
1 cup unflavored yoghurt
1 teaspoon ground cumin, toasted in a small ungreased skillet over low heat for 30 seconds

1. With a small, sharp knife, peel the cucumber and slice it lengthwise into halves. Scoop out the seeds by running the tip of a teaspoon down the center of each half.

2. Cut the cucumber lengthwise into ⅛-inch-thick slices, then crosswise into ½-inch pieces.

3. Combine the cucumber, onions and salt in a small bowl, and mix them together thoroughly with a spoon.

4. Let the mixture rest at room temperature for 5 minutes or so, then squeeze the cucumbers gently between your fingers to remove the excess liquid.

5. Drop the cucumber pieces into a deep bowl, add the tomato and coriander, and toss them together gently but thoroughly.

6. Combine the yoghurt and cumin and pour it over the vegetables, turning them about with a spoon to coat them evenly.

7. Taste for seasoning, cover tightly, and refrigerate for at least 1 hour, or until completely chilled, before serving.

Fresh Vegetables

The wise selection of fresh vegetables takes considerable expertness. The U.S. Department of Agriculture grades vegetables only at the wholesale level. (A bag of potatoes sometimes has U.S. Fancy or U.S. No. 1, the two top grades, printed on it, but this is just about the only evidence of grading that appears at the retail level.) Wholesale grading ensures minimum standards of quality; it is up to the customer to find the freshest and most flavorful vegetables.

As a rule, young vegetables are the tenderest and best-tasting; the biggest vegetable is not likely to be the best. Be sure to look most carefully at the part of the vegetable that counts. Wilted tops of beets and carrots are unimportant if the roots have good shape, texture and color. The leaves of spinach and lettuce are the important part; buy only clean, fresh-looking ones. In asparagus, the stalks are what count; they should be green the entire length with closed tips at the end. Freshness is important to both flavor and quality in all vegetables, so buy in quantities that you can use in a relatively short time.

Most fresh vegetables should be kept in the refrigerator, in the vegetable drawer or compartment designed for them, or covered in the lower part of the refrigerator. Ripe tomatoes, unhusked corn, unshelled lima beans and peas in the pod should be refrigerated but not covered. Sort all vegetables before storing and discard any that show decay. Wash them if they are very dirty but dry them well. If possible, simply shake the dirt off or wipe them clean before storing. Take care that lettuce and other greens are dry before storing; otherwise they will lose their crispness. It is best to wash and dry them just before using.

There are a few vegetables that should not be stored in the refrigerator: potatoes, dry onions, rutabagas, turnips, parsnips, hard-rind squash and eggplant. These should be stored at a cool temperature, around 60°; a cellar or utility room is a good place for this kind of storage. Onions and potatoes sprout at a high room temperature and soon deteriorate. Onions should be stored in loosely woven bags, potatoes in a dry, dark place with good air circulation. Both should be bought in small quantities if this kind of storage is unavailable.

Here is what to look for when selecting fresh vegetables:

ROOT VEGETABLES: In beets, carrots, parsnips, radishes, turnips and rutabagas, look for smooth, firm well-shaped roots. The color should be good and characteristic for the vegetable. Any flabbiness, moist spots or shriveling indicates decay or age.

In case of carrots and radishes remove both tips and tops before storing; they drain needed moisture from the root if left on. Remove the tops of beets but not the tips, lest they lose color and moisture.

LEAFY GREEN VEGETABLES: This group includes the cooking greens – chard, kale, collards and spinach; and the salad greens – leaf-type lettuce, chicory, escarole and watercress. The leaves should be clean and fresh-looking, and have a characteristic green color. Seedstalk, or sprouting, on any of these vegetable means age and it may show toughness. Too many wilted leaves or discolorations should be avoided.

ARTICHOKES: They should be globular, plump and heavy, with tight-fitting green scales. Size has little relation to an artichoke's flavor or quality.

ASPARAGUS: As said before, the tenderest asparagus is green along its entire stalk. Firm, closed tips are a sign of freshness.

BEANS AND PEAS: Look at the pods of these vegetables. In snap and yellow beans, they should be crisp and tender, filled with very immature seeds. The pods of lima beans should be fresh, dark green and well filled with plump beans. Pea pods should be a light green color with a soft texture and filled with well-developed peas. Once shelled, both limas and green peas should be used immediately; their flavor and quality fade quickly in the open air.

BROCCOLI AND CAULIFLOWER: The flower clusters should be compact and firm and not dried out. Broccoli bud clusters range from dark green to purplish-green and their stalks should be tender and firm. Good cauliflower flowerets are white or creamy-white and the outer leaves of the cauliflower should look fresh and green.

CABBAGE AND BRUSSELS SPROUTS: The best heads of cabbage should be solid and relatively heavy for their size, with stems trimmed close to the head and leaves that show little or no discoloration. Brussels sprouts are tiny cabbages that should be firm to the touch and have a bright green color.

CELERY: Crisp, clean stalks of medium length are the best. Test to see that they are brittle; avoid stalks that are discolored around the heart and leaves.

CORN: Milky, well-developed kernels are important. Husks should be a fresh-looking green, and still moist enough to fit firmly around the cob. Avoid corn with brown, mushy kernels at the tip of the ear.

CUCUMBERS: The freshest cucumbers are shiny, bright green and firm to the touch. Avoid yellowing or puffy ones.

EGGPLANT: A desirable one is dark purple and feels firm and heavy, with no bruises or cuts on the smooth skin.

GARLIC: A good bulb of garlic is one with plump cloves compactly set in an unbroken outer skin. Cloves that are sprouting and shriveled or have a broken skin are of poor quality.

ICEBERG LETTUCE: Easily packed and shipped, iceberg lettuce is the most widely available variety. It leaves should be crisp and bright-colored and in a fairly firm shape. "Rust" and small, jagged brown spots on the inner leaves are not good signs.

MUSHROOMS: Clean, preferably without any scars or browning, the best are a good white or creamy-white, with their caps completely closed so that no gills can be seen between the cap and the stem.

ONIONS: Green, fresh tops with necks white 2 or 3 inches up from the root are the marks of the choicest green onions, scallions and leeks. Dry, mature onions should be globular in shape, bright with dry skins. Moisture at the neck or on the outer skins is a sign of probable decay.

POTATOES: The best are firm, fairly smooth and free from eyes, with a regular shape for the variety. "New" potatoes bruise easily, and they do not keep well; "late" or "old" potatoes are more durable. Avoid mottled, leathery or scarred potatoes.

PEPPERS: Both sweet and hot peppers should look shiny, have a strong red or green color depending on their variety and be fairly firm to the touch.

SQUASH: There are many species, divided into two general kinds to shop for: summer and winter. Summer squash, which include zucchini and White Bush Scallop, are best when immature with a soft rind. Feel to see that they are heavy for their size and not bruised or discolored. Winter squash such as Butternut and Acorn have a hard rind. The rinds should be free of soft spots because these squash decay easily.

TOMATOES (technically a fruit, but sold and eaten as a vegetable): The best ones are ripened on the vine but this is often impractical for packing and shipping. They should, however, have begun to turn red before picking. Check for a plump shape with a general red color and a skin free from cracks or scars. If still hard, ripen them at home at room temperature out of the sun.

Sculpted Vegetables That Serve as Food and Garnish

BAMBOO-SHOOT TREES
With a sharp paring knife, trim shoots into triangular wedges. Make 4 or 5 V-shaped grooves lengthwise on two sides of the triangle. Slice into ⅛-inch-thick "tree-shaped" pieces.

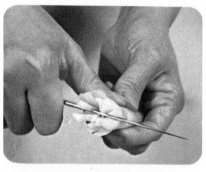
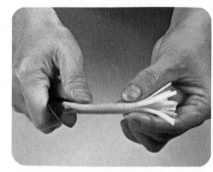

SCALLION BRUSHES
Trim root; cut off top, leaving 3 inches of firm stalk. Hold stalk firmly; make four crossing cuts 1 inch deep into one end. Repeat at other end. Place in ice water.

TOMATO ROSES
Peel a ripe, firm tomato to make a continuous strip of skin. Coil the strip, and in the palm of one hand spread the "petals" to form a rose shape with the other hand.

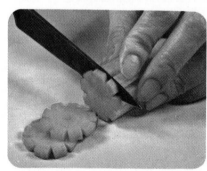

CARROT FLOWERS
Clean and peel the skin off a thick carrot. Cut V-shaped grooves lengthwise, spaced equally all around the carrot. Slice into ⅛-inch-thick pinwheels.

ICICLE RADISH FLOWERS
Peel and groove an icicle radish; trim one end into a cone. Using cone surface as guide, make very thin parings. Overlap ends of slice into flower cups. Refrigerate in ice water.

From top right, scallion brushes, carrot and icicle-radish flowers, radish fans and bamboo-shoot trees surround a carved tomato rose.

Herbs and Spices

HERBS are the leaves – or the seeds and flowers – of aromatic plants. Fresh herbs are preferable because once dried they may lose their aroma. If dried herbs are used they should be freshly dried, and should not be used in cold dishes until they have been soaked or cooked. In general, use about half as much of a dried herb as a fresh one. Herbs should be stored in airtight containers, and these must be kept in a cool place.

SPICES are the roots, barks, stems, buds, seeds or fruit of aromatic tropical plants. They should be bought in small quantities; they tend to lose their flavor quickly.

ALLSPICE: Not a blend of spices but a dried berry; its fragrance suggests a mixture of cinnamon, cloves and nutmeg. Available either ground or whole. Use the whole berries in soups, broths and gravies; use ground allspice in vegetables, cookies and cakes.

BASIL: The fresh or dried leaves of this herb are especially suited to most tomato dishes, as well as vegetables, meats, fish and salads.

BAY LEAF: This strong herb, also known as *laurel leaf,* enhances soups, meat stews and pot roasts and is part of a *bouquet garni.*

CARAWAY: A small, brown herb seed, caraway is found in rye bread and is also good in sauerkraut, cheeses, and soups and stews.

CARDAMOM: This sweet black spice is available ground or as a whole seed, in or out of its pod. It is used widely in Danish pastries. Try it also in spiced wines, fruit compotes, sauerbraten, pickles and curry.

CHERVIL: One of France's *fines herbes,* this lacy leaf enhances soups, green salads, potato salad, and egg and fish dishes.

CHIVES: The most delicate member of the onion family, and the only one that is considered an herb. The chopped slender leaves give a delicate onion accent to green salads, egg and fish dishes, soups and light sauces.

CINNAMON: This pungent spice comes either in sticks or as reddish-brown ground cinnamon. Use the sticks in pickling or sugar syrups; use ground cinnamon in baking, with cooked fruits and on puddings.

CLOVE: The nail-shaped whole clove is the traditional spice used for studding smoked ham. Ground cloves are used to flavor spice cakes, sweet potatoes and carrots.

CURRY POWDER: A prepared blend of from four to 40 spices, usually including turmeric, ginger, coriander, cumin, cloves and mustard. It is added to all curries, and frequently to some egg, seafood or vegetable dishes.

DILL: This herb is available packaged as seeds or weed, or fresh, as leaves. Use the seeds with fish and chicken. The weed or fresh leaves are excellent with tomatoes, potatoes, fish, in salads and cream sauces.

FENNEL: Use the whole seeds of this herb with fish or chicken, in breads, rolls and apple pies, marinades and spaghetti sauce.

GINGER: The ginger plant root has a hot, sweet flavor; it is available as a whole, ground or cracked spice. Bits of ginger root, found in Oriental or Spanish stores, are used in pickling, marinades and preserves. Ground ginger, more common, is used in baking, meat and poultry dishes.

MACE: A spice that is the lacy covering of the nutmeg shell, it has a less delicate flavor than nutmeg. Use ground mace in pound cake, puddings and in fish sauces.

MARJORAM: The leaves of this versatile herb of the mint family can be used whole or ground in poultry stuffing, tomato dishes, salads, green vegetables and with meats.

MINT: The leaves of the spearmint and peppermint herbs add a fresh, cool flavor to sauces for lamb and veal, to peas or carrots, frozen desserts, cold drinks and fruits.

MUSTARD: Two main varieties of mustard – white or yellow, and brown or Oriental – are grown as spices. Dry, powdered mustard can be used in sauces, salad dressings and cheese dishes. The tiny whole mustard seeds go into pickles and vegetable relishes.

NUTMEG: Available as a whole or ground spice. Freshly grated whole nutmeg seed is best. Use it in desserts, in breads or cakes, sprinkled on vegetables and on eggnog.

OREGANO: Also called wild marjoram. Use the whole leaves or ground herb in pizza, pasta, tomato dishes, and with vegetables and eggs.

PAPRIKA: Most of the paprika used in the U.S. is bright red in color and has a mild, sweet flavor. Hungarian paprika is less vivid but has more of a bite. This spice can be used to garnish light-colored foods and to flavor fish, meat and poultry, as well as goulash.

PARSLEY: This herb is available fresh in two varieties: curly-leaf and flat-leaf (also called Italian). Chopped fresh parsley is one of the *fines herbes,* and the sprigs are part of a *bouquet garni.* It is an attractive garnish and adds a pleasant taste to stuffings, soups, salads, meat and fish dishes.

PEPPER (BLACK AND WHITE): Black peppercorns are dried, unripened berries. White peppercorns are the pale kernel from a fully ripened peppercorn (the dark outer hull has been removed). Black pepper, available whole, cracked or ground, has a strong, hot taste. This spice is best in the freshly ground form for salads, vegetables and indeed almost any food. For light-colored sauces use white pepper, whole or ground.

PEPPER (RED): Ground or crushed red pepper (unrelated to either white or black) and ground Cayenne are available singly or as a blend. In varying shades of red, these spices have a hot, strong flavor. Use them sparingly in sauces for seafood, pizza and pasta.

ROSEMARY: The spiky leaves of this fragrant herb are excellent with lamb, beef and pork, green beans or boiled potatoes.

SAFFRON: The most expensive spice, it is available powdered or in threads, which must be crushed with the back of a spoon or with a mortar and pestle. Saffron is used sparingly for its golden color and its somewhat bitter flavor in many rice and fish dishes, curries and stews.

SAGE: The gray-green leaves of this herb are dried and are available whole, rubbed or ground. It is used widely in poultry and fish stuffings and with pork and veal.

SAVORY: There are two varieties, summer and winter savory. Summer savory is more common and more aromatic. Both herbs are available as whole or ground leaves and are used in poultry stuffings, dried bean and pea dishes, and meat loaf.

SESAME SEED: This spice is the dried, hulled fruit of a tropical plant, and is the source of a cooking oil used widely in the East. It is sold whole and untoasted, and can be baked on rolls, breads and buns. Toasted, it can garnish salads and cooked noodles.

TARRAGON: This herb is available fresh or as dried leaves. It is a must in *béarnaise* sauce and is also good with *eggs*, poultry or fish and sprinkled over a green salad.

THYME: An herb with strongly aromatic gray-green leaves, it is available whole or powdered. Use fresh in a *bouquet garni,* and in clam chowder, poultry stuffings and in almost any meat stew.

INDEX